Planning Your Career
Through Intense Interests

by the same authors

The Autism and Neurodiversity Self Advocacy Handbook
Developing the Skills to Determine Your Own Future
Yenn Purkis and Barb Cook
ISBN 978 1 78775 575 8
eISBN 978 1 78775 576 5

of related interest

Autism Working
A Seven-Stage Plan to Thriving at Work
Michelle Garnett and Tony Attwood
ISBN 978 1 78775 983 1
eISBN 978 1 78775 984 8

The Autism-Friendly Guide to Self-Employment
Robyn Steward
ISBN 978 1 78775 532 1
eISBN 978 1 78775 533 8

Autism Equality in the Workplace
Removing Barriers and Challenging Discrimination
Janine Booth
Foreword by John McDonnell
ISBN 978 1 84905 678 6
eISBN 978 1 78450 197 6

Planning Your Career Through Intense Interests

Yenn Purkis and Barb Cook

Jessica Kingsley Publishers
London and Philadelphia

First published in Great Britain in 2023 by Jessica Kingsley Publishers
An imprint of John Murray Press

1

Copyright © Yenn Purkis and Barb Cook 2023

The right of Yenn Purkis and Barb Cook to be identified as the
Author of the Work has been asserted by them in accordance
with the Copyright, Designs and Patents Act 1988.

A CIP catalogue record for this title is available from the
British Library and the Library of Congress

ISBN 978 1 83997 352 9
eISBN 978 1 83997 353 6

Printed and bound in Great Britain by Clays Ltd

Jessica Kingsley Publishers' policy is to use papers that are natural,
renewable and recyclable products and made from wood grown in
sustainable forests. The logging and manufacturing processes are expected
to conform to the environmental regulations of the country of origin.

Jessica Kingsley Publishers
Carmelite House
50 Victoria Embankment
London EC4Y 0DZ

www.jkp.com

John Murray Press
Part of Hodder & Stoughton Limited
An Hachette UK Company

Contents

INTRODUCTION. 7

1. What Is Autism? 11

2. Different Types of Jobs and Workplaces. 19

3. Career Planning Using Interests. 29

4. Harnessing Skills and Interests 47

5. Job Hunting: From Planning and Goal Setting to
   Getting and Starting Your New Job. 65

6. Positives of Autistic Staff/Business Owners – and
   Challenging Assumptions 111

7. Challenges and Barriers to Employment. 119

8. Personality Traits and Types: Using These to
   Your Advantage 125

9. Other Strategies, Tips and Thoughts around
   Employment 131

10. Understanding and Managing Workplace
    Relationships. 137

CONCLUSION. 167

GLOSSARY/LANGUAGE 169

Introduction

Hi readers,

We are Yenn Purkis and Barb Cook. We are autistic authors, advocates, employees and business owners. We want to share some of our knowledge with you to help you use your passionate interests (or 'special interests' or 'intense interests') to help you to build your career. We are both passionate about employment, particularly for autistic folks. A positive experience of the workplace is amazing. Work can provide meaningful and enjoyable activity, a sense of being part of something bigger, financial independence, a feeling of being part of the world and social connectedness, an income – and lots of other good things. Autistic people need everything we can get to support our entry into the workplace. This book intends to support autistic young adults – you – to plan your career based on what you love and have a passion for. For many people work is a bit of a bore, but, for an autistic person working in an area they are passionate about, work can be exciting, engaging and very enjoyable.

This book is all about work for autistic young people. It will help you to understand what your skills and strengths are and how you can use your interests and passions to drive a great career.

The book will explain how to career plan based on your passionate interests. It is all about how you can use the things you love to do and have an interest in to make a career – either in your own business or employed by someone else. Autistic people have amazing talents and skills, and you can use these passions and intense interests to make a great career.

Both authors are autistic and both of us have some wonderful passions which we use every day in our work. Doing work based on passion is an amazing thing and not only does it make autistic people great employees, it also translates into a world of work which is enjoyable and interesting for us.

Autistic people can struggle in the workplace for several reasons. Selection processes such as interviews can mean autistic people face challenges even before they start work. However, the world of employment does not need to be closed to autistic folks. Not only can we benefit from having a job or business, our employers or customers can also benefit from our passions and knowledge.

This book contains some helpful advice to enable you to turn your passion into a career and use your interests to drive a working life which is enjoyable and rewarding. Full of advice and activities, this book will help you to engage with the world of work and find work which you actually enjoy. It is all about seeing autism as a difference rather than a set of problems and negatives. Autistic people can achieve amazing things, especially when we believe in ourselves and draw on our passions and skills.

The book has a range of topics to help you harness your passions and interests, including goal and vision setting, identifying your skills and personality attributes, looking at what makes a positive workplace, common attributes of autistic employees and business owners, and challenging assumptions, to name just a few! This book will help you to understand yourself and your skills, think about and plan your career and understand how to harness your passions to build a career. We hope you enjoy it and that it helps you in your work journey.

CHAPTER ONE

What Is Autism?

Autism can be seen as a difference in how the brain is wired, affecting people in a range of ways. Autism is sometimes called a 'neurodivergent condition'. Other neurodivergent conditions include attention deficit disorder (ADD)/attention deficit hyperactivity disorder (ADHD), dyslexia, dyspraxia, Tourette's and synaesthesia. While historically autism has been viewed as a deficit or a problem, in recent times a different approach has gained influence – the idea of neurodiversity. This basically means that autistic people are 'different, not less' when compared with other people who are not autistic.

Autism is different for each person who is autistic. However, many autistic people share common attributes. These may include – but not be limited to:

- Differences in the way we communicate. Autistic people and neurotypical people (i.e., those without a diagnosis of a neurodivergent condition like autism, ADHD or dyslexia) tend to communicate differently. This does not mean the autistic person – or the neurotypical person for that matter – is communicating 'wrong', just differently. This can mean that neurotypical people assume an autistic person is being difficult when in fact they are just trying to be understood. The differences in communication can be seen as one of the key differences between autistic and neurotypical people.

- Having a logical approach to life. Autistic people tend to be very logical and when something is seen as illogical we might dismiss it. Neurotypical people often don't share this logical approach to life.

- A literal interpretation of conversations and situations. Autistic people tend to interpret things literally. It can mean we struggle with understanding what others are talking about.

- Social phobia. Autistic people may find social situations challenging – especially those involving communicating with neurotypical people. We can find being in groups of people (such as at a party) very difficult. Many autistic people like having friends but still find social situations challenging.

- Anxiety. Autistic people very frequently experience anxiety, especially in new situations.

- Fear of trying something new. Many autistic people like to do the same things over again. One of the authors of this book doesn't like to watch new movies but prefers to watch things they have seen before repeatedly, as this makes them feel more comfortable.

- Sensory processing issues. This means that sensory experiences can be significantly heightened. This can be both a good thing and a bad one. We might find lights too bright or sounds distracting and unpleasant. Or we might absolutely love shiny things.

- Hyper-empathy. This means people pick up on the emotions of those around them and are highly sensitive to emotional input.

- Overload, meltdown or shutdown. Autistic people can be sensitive to overload, especially where there is a lot of input – such as too much sensory, social or emotional input – they get overloaded and this needs to somehow get released. Meltdowns and shutdowns happen when a person cannot de-escalate that overload. A meltdown or shutdown can be different for each person. Autistic people almost always do not want to have a meltdown or shutdown and often feel guilty or upset when one happens. The best strategy for managing meltdowns and shutdowns is learning to spot the early warning signs and build in some de-escalation strategies. These strategies might include removing yourself from stressful or overloading situations or listening to relaxing music. Each person will have different strategies that work for them.

- Difficulties reading facial expressions or understanding what facial expressions mean.

- Prosopagnosia ('face blindness'). Many autistic people struggle to remember or recognize faces. Face blindness is not really known about by many people, so saying that you don't recognize faces might sound odd to someone who hasn't come across this condition before. It is a genuine issue and can be quite stressful. Many people try and figure out who they are talking with via the context of the conversation as they worry people will judge them if they say they couldn't remember their face. It is often easier to tell people about your prosopagnosia than not.

- Need for routine. Many autistic people thrive on structure and routine; it makes the world less confusing to navigate. Changes in routine can be very stressful and result in meltdown and shutdown.

- Pathological demand avoidance ('PDA'). This means that requests, demands or questions are viewed as traumatic and demanding. PDA is often called a 'profile' of autism. Some – but not all – autistic people have PDA. The PDA Society of the UK describes the PDA profile as

  > ...often anxiety related, are driven to avoid everyday demands and expectations (including things that they want to do or enjoy) to an extreme extent, tend to use approaches that are 'social in nature' in order to avoid demands, tend not to respond to conventional parenting, teaching or support approaches.[1]

- More likely to be transgender/gender-divergent. There is research evidence which demonstrates that up to 15 per cent of autistic people are trans and/or gender-divergent.[2]

- Passionate interests. Many autistic people are highly passionate about a topic and will happily spend all their time on it. Passions can be a variety of different

1   https://www.pdasociety.org.uk/what-is-pda-menu/about-autism-and-pda, accessed 13 November 2021

2   Organization for Autism Research (2020) 'Support for autistic transgender and gender diverse adults.' https://researchautism.org/support-for-autistic-transgender-and-gender-diverse-adults, accessed 13 November 2021

things depending on the person. One of the authors of this book has been passionate about fungi, cats, Dr Who, communism, art and autism advocacy! In fact, their latest passion on autism advocacy has resulted in them writing 12 books, giving a TED talk and lots of other things which would not have happened if their passion wasn't so strong. This attribute is actually what this book is based on! Our passionate interests can drive a number of positive things, including – as you will discover through reading this book – our jobs, businesses and careers.

- 'Stimming' – such as playing with a fidget toy, flapping hands, etc. Some people try to tell autistic people that stimming is bad. This is not true. As long as stims aren't destructive or harmful then they are actually a great way to manage anxiety and demonstrate excitement or happiness too.

- Difficulties with eye contact. Autistic people often struggle with making eye contact. Sometimes people tell them that they have to and force them to make eye contact despite it being stressful and experienced as invasive. In fact, eye contact is not necessary for communication – if it was then nobody would be able to communicate using a telephone!

- Honesty. Autistic people tend to be very honest and often struggle to lie even if it might protect them if they do. This honesty can be seen as a very positive attribute.

- Fear of mistakes/perfectionism. This can be very challenging for autistic people. We might worry about getting something wrong at school or work and find it hard to let go, even for things which probably don't matter much in the scheme of things.

- Tendency for burnout. Burnout occurs when a person is overloaded – this overload can relate to a number of factors including work, relationships, social communication or demands (especially for people with pathological demand avoidance). Burnout can be debilitating and make it difficult for people to engage in things they enjoy or need to do.

- Deep understanding of animals and nature. Many – but not all – autistic people have a strong intuitive connection to nature and particularly to animals. An assistance animal or pet can be the difference between an autistic person being miserable and not coping and being able to navigate the world well.

- Creativity. Despite stereotypes that suggest autistic people lack creativity, in fact many autistic people are highly creative and excel at art, music, writing and/or acting.

- Being 'gifted'. Autistic people are often gifted or 'twice exceptional' and have a high level of skills in one or more areas. This can also be related to passionate interests where an autistic person is fascinated with a topic and develops a high level of knowledge and skills in this area.

- Thinking 'outside the box'. Many autistic people think in a way that neurotypical people do not. They can pick up on things that others miss. This makes autistic people highly sought after in some areas, such as some workplaces or in academia.

More about autism

Autism is not acquired. What this means is that a person is born autistic. It is not possible to fix or cure autism. In fact, many autistic people don't want to be 'fixed' and like and value themselves just as they are. Autistic people often get along well with other autistic or neurodivergent people. This is because as autistic people we are like people from a different culture. Imagine if you went to live in a different country. You learn the language and the customs, but it is never quite like home. If someone from your home country visits you then it is likely that you will get along so much better with them because they understand you like nobody from your adopted country can. The person from your homeland speaks your language and shares knowledge and customs with you. This is very similar to being amongst other autistic people. Our autistic peers speak our 'language' and share knowledge and experience with us. That said, autistic people do not necessarily get along with all other autistic people. We are all individuals, but it is often the case that autistic and neurodivergent people get along better with one another than with neurotypical folks.

ACTIVITY

What are some of your autistic attributes? Do you like them, dislike them or not really mind about them one way or another?

Being proud of who you are

There is a concept which you may well have heard of called neurodiversity. Neurodiversity is the idea that everyone's brains are different and that this is perfectly OK. The idea of neurodiversity sees this as being a natural part of being human and states that autistic people are simply different, not deficient or somehow broken.

A neurodiversity approach makes it possible for autistic people to like and value ourselves. The idea of autistic pride comes from the idea of neurodiversity. Autistic pride enables autistic people to be confident and proud of who we are. Being autistic – and being disabled generally – usually results in a lot of questions about a person's value in society as well as stereotypes and assumptions. Autistic pride and neurodiversity are things which challenge the negative assumptions and stereotypes about autism. We have the right to be proud of who we are. Autistic pride makes the world easier to navigate for autistic people. It also gives us the opportunity to educate and support others to understand our reality and appreciate us for who we are.

ACTIVITY
Are there things which make you feel proud to be who you are? What are these and why do they make you feel proud?

CHAPTER TWO

Different Types of Jobs and Workplaces

Introduction to employment – types of jobs and workplaces

There are many kinds of jobs, industries and workplaces out there. Some jobs suit some people better than others. Knowing what kind of industry and workplace you want to work in can help you to find a job that suits you well. Sometimes we have a view that working in one industry or job will be terrible, but in fact if we actually experienced it we might find that we really enjoy it. Conversely sometimes we might think a job is suited to us when in fact it isn't.

An industry refers to an overarching category which includes several different kinds of job. Examples include hospitality, agriculture, government administration, tourism, education, health services or entertainment, 'Jobs' refers to the kinds of work within an industry. For example, chefs, wait staff, bar staff and dishwashers all work in the hospitality industry. Similarly, teachers, lecturers, teachers' aides and school administrators work in the education industry. The jobs can be quite varied within each industry. You might find one job in an industry really appeals to you while another job in the same industry doesn't suit you at all.

Some people might tell you that autistic people are only suited to a limited number of jobs and that many industries are not 'autism friendly'. In fact, autistic people can be found in all industries. It is about finding work that suits you as an individual rather than applying stereotypes and assumptions to autistic people and our capability to work in a particular type of place. When author Yenn applied for a job in the Australian Public Service in 2006, their autistic mentor warned them against it saying that the public service was not 'autism friendly'. Yenn ignored the advice and took the job. They are working in the public service to this day, more than 15 years later. Assumptions do not help autistic people. We are all different and that is OK. In fact, it is more than OK – it is excellent.

Jobs in different industries

This section lists a selection of industries and examples of some of the jobs within them. It is not an exhaustive list but gives an overview of some of the jobs available in each industry.

Information and communication technology (ICT)
Jobs in this industry include: computer programmer, technical support, software analyst, web developer, game designer, information security analyst, systems analyst, IT consultant.

Hospitality
Jobs in this industry include: chef, cook, wait staff, dishwasher, kitchen hand, hotel receptionist/concierge.

Retail

Jobs in this industry include: retail manager, shop assistant, store person, packer.

Government administration

Jobs in this industry include: policy adviser, human resources practitioner, auditor, government lawyer, senior executive, project manager.

Education

Jobs in this industry include: teacher, university lecturer, teacher's aide, school administrator, tutor.

Health care

Jobs in this industry include: nurse, doctor, psychologist, assistant in nursing, occupational therapist, dietitian, exercise physiologist, physiotherapist, speech therapist, occupational therapist.

Entertainment

Jobs in this industry include: musician, visual artist, comedian, actor, screenwriter, author.

Tourism

Jobs in this industry include: tour guide, travel agent, hotel staff, airline staff.

Legal professions

Jobs in this industry include: barrister, solicitor, legal clerk, police officer, prison officer.

Agriculture

Jobs in this industry include: farmer, farm hand, market gardener, farm manager, fruit picker, vintner.

Construction

Jobs in this industry include: bricklayer, concreter, plumber, electrician, tiler, site manager, architect, engineer, carpenter, builder's labourer.

Fashion

Jobs in this industry include: fashion designer, stylist, textile designer, fashion model.

Hair and beauty

Jobs in this industry include: hairdresser, beauty therapist, masseur, nail technician.

Finance

Jobs in this industry include: tax agent, bank teller, financial planner, loan manager, share trader, superannuation fund manager, insurance agent.

Manufacturing

Jobs in this industry include: engineer, manufacturing technician, welder, assembler, factory hand.

Media

Jobs in this industry include: journalist, producer, video editor, social media manager, photographer, advertising executive, graphic designer.

Mining

Jobs in this industry include: miner, geologist, mining engineer, truck driver.

Transport

Jobs in this industry include: truck driver, train driver, tram driver, air traffic controller, bus driver, airline pilot, ferry pilot, taxi driver, ride share driver, flight attendant.

Real estate

Jobs in this industry include: real estate agent, property manager, receptionist/administration officer, conveyancer.

Sport and recreation

Jobs in this industry include: professional sportspeople, coach, personal trainer, stadium ground staff, club manager.

This list is not a complete list of every job in the world. Rather, it gives examples of some of the different jobs in different industries. You may have noticed that some similar jobs are included in different industries. This is because there is some overlap and some jobs do belong in more than one industry.

What does a positive workplace look like?

A positive workplace is one where people are able to do their jobs without prejudice, discrimination, bullying or harassment. A positive workplace supports diversity and inclusion for all its employees. Positive workplaces celebrate the achievements of their employees and give support to enable their staff to do their job well. Positive workplaces are autism and neurodiversity-friendly.

In a positive workplace, managers are available to talk to their staff and set reasonable tasks and deadlines. In a positive workplace if there are issues such as bullying and harassment, these are addressed promptly and effectively. Positive workplaces do not engage in unethical corporate conduct (such as criminal activity, fraud, etc.) and they allow employees to be represented by unions if they choose to be.

Micro-business, entrepreneurship and self-employment

Employment isn't always about working for someone. Some of us have a passion to turn our intense interests into a business. When working for yourself, you don't have to answer to a boss or co-workers as you are the one in charge. Many autistic/neurodivergent people have taken the plunge to become entrepreneurs. Autistic people often thrive on doing the research required to be successful, to evaluate the market they are taking on, plus it is an opportunity to show the world their creativity and flair.

Especially in the arts, design and fashion sectors, being quirky and different tends to be valued highly – the perfect example of how diversity can be expressed and explored within the workplace.

I too (author Barb) ventured into the self-employment realm when I finished my studies in graphic design back in the early 1990s. I touted myself as a freelance designer and within the first year I was designing for three different companies. I felt really impressed with myself as I could turn the work around at lightning speed, could do it at all hours of the day and wasn't restricted to a nine-to-five job.

However, we need to be careful that we don't work ourselves to extreme levels and long hours without taking the time to implement good working practices and self-care. This can take a toll on us, especially when we hyper-focus, having little concept of how much time has passed and knowing when to stop and take breaks. These are very important things to consider when working for yourself.

In the early days of working for myself, I would start a design project and sit there in front of my computer until I had finished it, ignoring the need to eat and those around me. The only time I would realize there was something outside the computer screen was when one of my cats would hang off my leg with their claws wanting their dinner. Oh, I would think, I had better eat too.

The other thing that we can tend to not be so savvy on is things relating to the 'boring stuff', like doing taxes, putting enough money away to pay bills, that sort of thing. We are so caught up in the work we love doing that the stuff that doesn't interest us can be pushed aside or feel incredibly challenging to start and complete, and we can literally switch off to its existence. We can end up not doing the very important work of running our business, paying our taxes and suppliers, or returning important emails and phone calls.

When going into working for ourselves we need to have a good team to support us. We need to have people to do all the stuff we are not interested in or good at, that allows us to primarily focus on our talents and what we create. But we also need to be mindful that we need to make money in the passion we are doing too.

Case study: Co-workers with passionate interests

Working with another person in business can be a great benefit. When I owned a video store for a few years with my business partner who is also autistic was an example of this. We worked incredibly well together as we both had very different skill-sets to offer and complemented each other by having a wider diversity of skills collectively. My partner was incredibly good at talking to people and telling them in great detail about what movies to watch. He would memorize each video store member's movie tastes and each time they came in, he would suggest great movies for them to watch. Everyone in the town knew him as the movie guy and that our store was the place to go. His intense knowledge around movies was incredible.

When we designed the store layout, we both looked at what would best interest the customer visually. With my design and art skills I could see what would catch people's eye in the layout. I painted the signage for the store and would print huge posters for the windows to entice customers to hire more videos. I also designed store flyers and my partner would print them. He knew how to use our little printing press. I designed, he printed. We were a great team!

You can see how combining talents and passion can make an excellent business enterprise. When we are passionate, know our product and feel confident in what we are offering, we can overcome things like social interaction a lot easier when we work in partnership. We can actually be excellent at customer service when we know and are passionate about our product and how we can best advise our customers in making choices of what to buy. We can give them that tailored touch as we take that extra time in recalling what they like or want.

Now one of the downsides on both our accounts was being naïve in trusting the sellers of videos. Believing their advice about what to buy for the store at times proved to be costly as the movies they would recommend and sell to us were B-grade movies and didn't rent very often. This would lead to us not making very much profit and not enough money to cover the running costs of the business that included paying rent for shop space, electricity, tax and staff wages. As autistic people we can believe and trust what people say to us. We believe what people say and often we never realized that they were in the business of selling as much product as possible to the buyer, which was us, and so they didn't come from a moralistic standpoint of telling you that a potential movie wasn't that great.

At times these poor business decisions did leave us in financial difficulties. Times were often tough, and because we put our soul into what we were doing, we found it hard to take time off or to relax. Just over three years later, we sold the business and vowed to never take on a business requiring us to work seven days a week again. We ended up very burnt out. However, we did learn a lot from the experience. We learnt that even working in a partnership, we still needed to engage in outside expert support to assist us with managing the financial aspect and running costs of the business and to do a lot more research ourselves on a product, rather than just taking the advice from our suppliers.

It really is a tough balance when implementing good business and self-care practices. It is OK to ask for support and advice when running your own business. As much as we want to be independent, we all need someone to help us along the way in this journey called life. We need to have other people to help us achieve our business vision and goals.

Remember, it doesn't matter how many people work with you or assist you; you are the person creating and building your dream business, and this can be incredibly rewarding.

CHAPTER THREE

Career Planning Using Interests

How do you know what you want to do?

It can be difficult to decide what you want to do for your career. You might really love something but not be aware of how to turn it into a career. Or you might simply be unable to decide what you want to do. This book is all about helping you to figure out what your plans around work might be and how to turn your interests and passions into a meaningful career.

Most autistic people will have a passionate or 'intense' interest. These are things which we love and find engaging. An autistic person can be motivated by our passionate interests and they can become the basis for a career. This makes a lot of sense, as doing a job based in something you love is a very good idea. It means you can not only pursue your interest, but you can also use your interest to earn money and spend your time at work doing something you enjoy.

Autistic passions can take many forms. The authors have met autistic people with a range of passionate interests including politics, fungi, photography, air conditioners, autism advocacy, anime and Star Wars. Most autistic people will have at least one topic that they are passionate about and many of us go through a range of interests during our lifetimes.

Turning your passionate interest into a career is a great thing to do and can mean you spend your working life doing things you love and are motivated to do.

Knowing what you want to do for a career can be challenging but basing it in your passionate interest is a great starting point. This book will provide advice and support for autistic young people to use their passions to create a career – or careers – for themselves which is rewarding and enjoyable.

It is important to be aware that most people have a number of careers over their lifetime. You may start out doing something and do that for a while and then change to something else. This is perfectly OK. If you start to do one thing and it doesn't work out, then you can move into doing something else. It is also perfectly OK to spend your entire career doing the same or similar things. One of the authors of this book has a close friend who has been working in the same job for almost 30 years! They have no intention of changing jobs and love what they do.

Working out what you want to do for work may take a while. You can discover your preferred career through testing out some work activities and seeing which ones work for you and which don't.

What should I do?

Deciding on a career path doesn't have to start early and does not have to be set in stone. If you are just starting out on your employment path, ask yourself, what am I passionate about, and compile a list. This list does not have to be employment focused. It can be hobbies you enjoy, types of books you like to read, your preference between writing or speaking. Do you enjoy writing creatively or in a journalistic style? Are you introverted or extroverted? Many autistic people are introverted, but find when they are doing something they love, they can become extroverted.

There are a number of passionate interests which many autistic people share and which can quite naturally translate into a rewarding career path. These include:

Music

If you have an interest or passion for music – as many autistic people do – this can translate into a range of career options. Many autistic people have sensitive hearing and can identify the smallest of differences in sounds. This is often called 'perfect pitch'. You may hear a piano out of key or can sing the scales on point! However, there can be some challenges when working in a music career.

There can be lots of competition, especially if you are considering being a singer. There can be many hours of practice needed each day and only a small number of people become highly successful. But don't let this put you off. You could be a backing singer for a band or sing jingles for radio and television advertisements. These types of roles can help you get a foot in the door of the music industry!

Music careers

- Touring musician.

- Classical musician.

- Recording artist.

- Backing singer.

- Music teacher.

- Hosting an online channel featuring different instruments or music styles.

- Working in a music shop.

- Composing music.

- Music journalist.

Gaming

If you have a passion for gaming – and let's face it, many of us do, you may want to take your passion and skills for playing games further by earning an income. You could be a beta tester for new and upcoming games or apps that companies develop. You can often find companies looking for testers to try out their new game or app before it gets released to the public. Or you could use your knowledge of games you play and work in a gaming store. You could gain experience by volunteering as a mentor or group leader in a local gaming group to help build your confidence and skills, plus learn about what other people enjoy about gaming and the wider variety of games that people play!

Gaming careers

- Professional gamer (on a platform such as Twitch).

- Game designer.

- Working in a shop that sells games.

- Game reviewer.

- Composing music for games.

- Programmer.

Science

If you have a passion for science, there are many career pathways you could take. If you continue onto university, you could get involved in research projects. There are many people involved in big research projects and it is a great way to take your first steps in understanding how research is conducted and how research can benefit the wider community. You may have an interest in rocks and a career as a geologist may interest you. Learning about how rocks are formed and how the landscape of the earth evolved can point you in the direction of using knowledge about rock formations in relation to climate events, the weather or volcanoes!

Science careers

- Pathologist.

- Palaeontologist.

- Archaeologist.

- Medical researcher.

- Forensic scientist.

- Academic/researcher.

- Science teacher.

- Statistician.

Film

Many autistic people have a passion for movies and film. Acting and drama allow for us to undertake a different persona. You may be great at remembering lines or repeating back phrases you hear. Working in this industry can be exciting and we can practise communication and relationship skills through acting too! Start small by applying as a movie extra in a local production or gain experience by joining your local theatre company or drama group.

Film and movie careers

- Actor/extra.

- Directing films.

- Composing music for movies.

- Screenwriting.

- Producing.

- Casting agent.

- Providing technical support for films (e.g., electricians or sound technicians).

- Film reviewer/journalist.

Art, design, illustration and creative writing

A lot of autistic people love comics, anime and graphic novels. These can translate into some great careers. You can practise your writing or design skills by creating your own blog and publish content about one of your areas of interest. This can build your creative skills and potentially build an online audience that will visit your website. If you love drawing and illustrating, start putting together a portfolio of your work. This will become a crucial part when applying for jobs in the creative industries as many employers will want to see examples of your creations.

Creative careers

- Cartoonist.

- Working in the publishing industry.

- Illustrator.

- Author.

- Working in a comic shop.

- Professional artist.

- Book illustrator.

- Graphic designer.

- Advertising professional.

- Art teacher.

- Art therapist.

- Interior designer.

Sports

Many autistic people love sports. A career in sport does not need to involve being a sportsperson (but it can too!). You may have a talent for writing up training plans that require consistent routines and repetition. Autistic people have a fantastic eye for detail, so you may have the edge on your competing team, for example, if you want to be a coach of a netball team. Sports require dedication, precision and skills and this may be a strength, especially if you are passionate about a sport you currently play or watch!

Sport and exercise careers

- Personal trainer.

- Coach.

- Sports journalist.

- Sportsperson.

- Bookmaker.

- Sports psychologist.

Animals

Many autistic people absolutely love animals and a career working with animals may appeal to many autists. To gain experience in working with animals, reach out to your local animal shelter or refuge as they are always needing volunteers to assist with feeding, cleaning, walking and caring for animals. You could consider becoming a wildlife carer; this can be rewarding in caring for your native wildlife and nursing them back to health.

Animal-based careers

- Veterinarian.

- Veterinary nurse.

- Dog trainer.

- Artist who makes pet portraits.

- Kennel hand.

- Customs/quarantine/police dog handler.

- Horse trainer.

- Jockey.

- Pet shop employee.

- Cat boarding facility staff member.

Trains/railways

A lot of autistic people love trains and railways. Working in the railway industry often requires a certain level of training, especially if you are considering driving the train. You may want to consider starting out working on the platform so that you can learn how the timetable runs at your local station. Positions often come up within the industry, so you may be able to work your way up the ladder to becoming a train driver. Also consider looking into traineeships that may come up when working in this industry as they can provide you with on-the-job training as well as further study at a college or university while you are working.

Railway careers

- Train driver.

- Station staff member.

- Train maintenance worker.

- Conductor.

- Ticket inspector.

- Creator of model railways.

- Railway line worker.

Planes

Many autistic people love planes and aviation. Working in aviation can be a highly rewarding career and you could travel the world too! If you are considering becoming a pilot or flight attendant, you will need extensive training, so be prepared to put in the hard work! However, if you enjoy travel and far off destinations, you may consider working in a travel agency where you could advise customers on exciting places to visit or interesting tours they could go on when they are on holiday!

Aviation careers

- Pilot.

- Flight attendant.

- Travel agent.

- Aviation engineer.

- Baggage handler.

- Ground staff.

- Customs officer.

- Quarantine officer.

When you have created a comprehensive list, you will start to see a pattern of preferences and styles that you have. Often, until we objectively write down and evaluate our values and passions, we don't realize that there may be employment pathways that we are suited to. This can even be to do with the food we eat! If you are a vegan/vegetarian for example, you certainly might not consider working as a butcher.

But there is also a flip side to this when you carefully consider your future. For example, it may initially appear to a person with strong environmental views that they would not be suited to working in the mining industry. These industries are often viewed negatively in environmental terms, but these very same industries have extremely high standards and legislation to abide by to minimize environmental damage to the surrounding land-scape. A person on the autism spectrum may be highly valued in a position as environmental safety officer at a mine due to their attention to detail, their moral views in upholding environmental laws and finding creative solutions with 'out of the box' thinking in how to reduce environmental impact.

Now, these very same strategies considering what employment best suits you work for people of all ages. If you have been job seeking or working for many years without job fulfilment or have had a variety of jobs that never worked out, taking these very steps of re-evaluating what is important to you and your values will help you to decide on how to approach your future career path.

As an autistic woman myself (Barb) who is now 53 years of age, I have finally found my passion in working in the field of employment and supporting my fellow autistic peers in finding contentment through the right job. After experiencing a lifetime of failed job positions and resigning myself to the fact that I would never hold down a long-term job, it wasn't until I received my diagnosis at mid-life over 13 years ago that I could re-eval-uate what I wanted to do and choose work that suited me and my neurology. I certainly didn't expect to be gaining my Master of Autism in Education and Employment degree at the age of 50. It goes to show, when we learn about ourselves and what works for us, we certainly can grow and flourish.

Can your preferred job change over time?

In a word, yes. Your preferred job can change over time. This can happen for several reasons including:

- Your interests change. Many autistic people's passionate interests change over time. You may be driven and motivated by a topic for a few years and then this may change, and you may be interested in something different, potentially leading to a career change. This is perfectly OK and quite common.

- You might start a job and realize it is not something you want to do. This is also OK, and many people change jobs or careers because they try something and realize it is not something they want to do, or they find something that they prefer to work on.

- You want to do something different. While some people are happy to do the same job for a long time, others want to try different things and test out other career paths. This is OK and quite common.

- You want to advance your career or win a promotion. Some people are happy to work at a particular level or in the same job long-term, but others want career advancement or promotion. This is true for autistic people too. While a lot of people think an autistic person should be grateful to have any job, this is in fact not the case. Autistic employees have the same right to career advancement and promotion, should they want it, as anyone else does. Just because a person is autistic does not mean that they should be satisfied to be at one level for their whole career – although there is nothing wrong with that if that is actually what they want to do.

About 'dream jobs'

Many people want a 'dream job'. But what actually is a dream job? Dream jobs are something which are quite subjective. In fact, seeking a 'dream job' may not be a very helpful way of approaching your career. Putting your focus on getting a 'dream job' can result in dissatisfaction with the job that you actually have or may mean you miss out on opportunities which might lead to a fantastic job because you are holding on for the perfect job.

You should actually be wary about the idea of 'dream jobs', as the potential for disappointment can be significant. It is better to make the most of the job you have and assess what you need to make it better than to pin your hopes on a specific dream job. Be aware that jobs change in time and you may end up in a great job without expecting to or, conversely, that you may secure what you think will be your dream job but instead be disappointed as it doesn't live up to your expectations.

There are many elements of a job which can be positive or negative and impact on our enjoyment of the job. Some of the elements of a job which can make it a great job include:

- the work itself and the tasks required to do your job

- your manager and in particular your relationship with your manager

- your relationship with your colleagues

- the physical workplace

(this includes the location of the building and how convenient it is to get there and the interior elements of the workplace like the lighting or noise level)

- access to adjustments to the workplace to support any need you may have (sensory, etc.)

- the opportunity to have control over what tasks you do

- whether you need to supervise staff

- recognition for good work

- the working hours

- the opportunity for promotion and career advancement

- the salary

- the nature of the working arrangement – e.g., casual, part-time, full-time, contractor, etc.

- the opportunity to do different things

- the opportunity to work from home or in other remote ways.

These elements can determine how we feel about our work and – if we are lucky – mean that our job is a great job. They can apply in having your own business or in working for an employer.

One of the big factors with success at work is how you feel towards your job. Two different people can have the same or a very similar set of circumstances in a workplace and have completely different attitudes to their job. As autistic people we can struggle with negative attitudes – ours and others' – and may focus only on the difficult parts of a situation. However, it is possible to change that and try to see the positives as well. This can be as easy as writing down all the things that are good about a situation or talking to others to gauge their thoughts on the situation, which might be different to your thoughts and opinions.

Even if you find a dream job, it does not necessarily mean that there will be no issues or challenges with it. Elements of your dream job may be unpleasant and this is actually OK. It helps to focus on positives rather than negatives. So, if your job, which is mostly very positive and inclusive, has some elements you don't like, it is best to reflect that you enjoy your job most of the time and that is a pretty good outcome. However, if you are being bullied at work or facing sexual harassment or other discrimination then that needs to be addressed. In such circumstances you can talk to your supervisor – unless they are the one doing the bullying or harassment in which case contacting their manager – if they have one – is a better approach. If your workplace has a human resources department you can raise complaints around bullying and harassment with them and if you are a member of the relevant union, you can also raise issues around bullying and harassment with them.

Breaking the stigma on autism and employment choices

Information technology (IT) has boomed over the past 30 years and become an integral part of the modern developed world. Employment opportunities in IT exploded alongside this growth and created pathways for many autistic people in finding job security in an industry that has been stigmatized as the place where the 'geeks' gravitate. Software giants headhunt talented autistic people for positions in program development and defending against cybercrimes. Autistic people have been pigeonholed that we are gifted and talented in computers, math and science. Certainly, some of us fit this role, but what about the millions of autistic and neurodivergent people globally who do not fit the misconception that we are all computer 'nerds'? Where are the jobs for these people?

Current media trends provided us with a starting point when thinking of potential industries and career pathways that autistic and neurodivergent people could embrace with a passion, outside the IT box. For example, Greta Thunberg's climate change protests ignited a global passion within the autistic community, showing our true depth of empathy, determination and the powerful interest that many autistic people have in environmental and sustainable practices. In her work, you can see the benefits of the neurological differences of autistic and neurodivergent people reflected in the difference of thought and analysis of global concerns. Autistic people can be passionate researchers, seeing patterns and connections in weather events, the changes in climate, the environmental design of our cities, consumerism and waste management, for example. This concern for the overall wellbeing of our fellow humankind, not only dispels, but smashes, some of the myths that stigmatize autistic people.

The catastrophic fires across Australia in 2019–2020 highlight another serious consideration of our environmental future within a country with climatic extremes. This unfortunate wake-up call sends a resounding message that we urgently need more people in roles of land management, sustainability and conservation to reduce the impact of devastating and destructive events. The deep empathy that many autistic people have for wildlife and nature needs to be embraced and career opportunities expanded in that space, to ensure countries around the world have a sensible and pragmatic approach in creating harmony between ecosystems and the consumer-based world we live in. The employment opportunities are immense when we steer away from the perception that autistic people are only suitable for IT roles.

These are some of the career pathways related to the environment and land management that we envision as a priority in our global future and where autistic people are likely to be well-placed:

- land care – forestry, agricultural technicians, land economists

- fire land management

- rangers

- conservation

- sustainability

- ecosystem management

- wildlife and fauna

- environmental planning

- alternative energies – solar, energy storage, wind

- public health and society – food and nutrition

- water sustainability and sanitation

- inspectors and regulators

- occupational and environmental health professionals

- legislators and public relations

- atmospheric scientists and meteorologists.

This is only a small sample of potential career pathways that autistic and neurodivergent people would excel in related to environmental protection. We can also put pressure on governing bodies, our leaders and businesses to expand on their current trajectory and to be part of embracing differences in thinking and to employ neurodiverse minds, that could potentially create a world that benefits all of society. This is a way in which autistic passions might not only lead to a career, but also change the world.

CHAPTER FOUR

Harnessing Skills and Interests

What skills do I need to get that job?

Each job requires a different set of skills. While you might think it is a bad idea to go for a job where you do not have all the required skills, in fact we often pick up new skills in the course of a job. Most managers do not expect their new starters to know how to do every aspect of their role.

Working out what skills we need can be a tricky thing to do. There is a fine line between going for a job we might be able to work into and choosing a role which is highly inappropriate. When considering the suitability of a new job, it can help to identify the main skills the job might entail. For example, working as a bricklayer would involve, first, a level of technical skill and some qualifications, but also the ability to do physical labour and work outdoors. It is also a job requiring specific qualifications. You can't just turn up and figure it out. Conversely, some jobs are more suited to picking up skills along the way. When one of the authors of this book was in their early 20s they got a job being an assistant at a gallery. The author had a passion for art and was interested in the business of the gallery. They were also computer literate and had worked in a customer-facing role before. The author loved this job and was very good at it. They recognized that their skill-set was relevant for this job and anything they needed to learn for the role could fairly easily be taught.

It may be helpful to ascertain what your skills actually are. It can be useful to do this with a friend or family member, especially one that has worked in a few different roles themselves. Things you may not realize are skills may actually be highly valuable in the workplace. A selection of skills includes:

- customer service experience

- gardening

- working well with people from diverse backgrounds

- respectful

- speaking other languages

- patience

- reliability

- ability to write code

- proficiency at Microsoft applications

- ability to spot errors

- art and graphic design skills

- ability to write well

- thoughtfulness

- resilience

- good with animals

- determination

- ability to follow instructions

- ethical approach to life

- honesty.

This is but a small selection of skills which might help enable you to do a job well.

Some skills are innate. These are sometimes called 'soft skills' or 'enabling skills'. They often relate to a person's character or personality. Some of the skills in the list above are 'soft skills' and some are practical skills related to doing a job. Contrary to the stereotype, autistic people often have a great set of soft skills. Soft skills are quite difficult to learn which is one reason managers tend to like a person who has some of these skills. Other skills, the more practical sort of skills, can be learned. This means if you start a job and you don't have all the practical skills you need, it is probably not going to be that difficult for you to pick them up. Author Yenn works in government administration for their day job, when they aren't writing or doing public speaking. When they started their job they had never used Microsoft Excel. They were terrified that their employer would terminate their employment due to them being unable to create or use an Excel spreadsheet but what actually happened was that their boss sent them on an Excel course – which was easier for everyone! They now enjoy using Excel and still have a job.

ACTIVITY

Identify and list some of the skills you have which might be useful in the workplace. If you like, identify which of the skills are enabling or 'soft' skills and which are more practical skills relating to doing a job.

What are your career ambitions?

Some of us may already know what our career ambitions are, but it is always good to revisit this. Our choices can change as we discover other careers that may be appealing to us or that we had never considered before until we saw an advertisement in the job market and thought, 'Hmm, I would like to do that'.

Some people have an intense interest, but they are not sure how that intense interest would fit into different types of jobs or roles. A person may be very specific in their interest or just have one job that they want to do, but this may not be achievable, so it is good to consider other roles where you could incorporate skills you have related to an area of interest.

If you do not know what you would like to do or would like to know about how your skills and strengths would match to particular industries, there are some resources that can help you with making a choice, including:

- myWay Employability Autism CRC: https://mywayemployability.com.au

- myfuture: https://myfuture.edu.au

- Do It Profiler: https://doitprofiler.com

- Genius Within: https://geniuswithin.org

- Autism Career Pathways: https://autismcareerpathways.org

- Underwing: https://underwingliverpool.com

- Neurodiversity in Business: https://neurodiversityinbusiness.org

- Lexxic: www.lexxic.com

Having a clear understanding of the type of career or job that you would like to do can help you in deciding what type of information to initially put in your resume. This can be especially beneficial when you currently don't have any job applications to apply for, but want to get your resume put together ready for when a potential suitable job application arises.

Work to your strengths: Suitable careers

When you have a neurodivergent mind it is important to recognize and learn what your strengths and challenges are, and how they may differ from other people around you.

There are some jobs that may be a better match for the type of neurology that you have. The key to this is to pick a career that makes the best use of your skills and strengths. That way your challenges won't create major issues. You can keep a few things in mind as you consider your future career or when changing your career.

Pick something you enjoy

Everyone does better in a job if their work sparks their interest and keeps them motivated. If you are bored and frustrated easily, it will be harder for you to stay on track at work. Before you pick a career, or if you are in a career that is not suiting you, you can make three lists. Make a list of what you're good at, a list of what you like to do, and a list of what someone else will pay you to do this career. Your ideal job should tick all of these three lists.

What I am good at	What I would like to do	How much will someone pay me to do this job?
Gardening	Work in a nursery	$20 per hour

Focus on your strengths

When looking for a job or changing careers it may be worth considering jobs that look for originality and unique ways to solve problems. So, jobs that involve innovative thinking can potentially be a great fit for your neurology. Examples include being an artist, an inventor, musician, a teacher or an advertising professional.

You may enjoy tasks that are repetitive or require a high level of attention to detail. Some examples of this type of work could be data entry, coding, security software development, scientist or research academic.

We also need to consider types of careers for brains that get bored or distracted easily. The upside is that you may thrive in jobs with constant change and quick pace. With every day at work being different or feeling different, you may feel more engaged and interested in doing your job. Some examples of this type of work include being a firefighter, police officer, paramedic, emergency room doctor or nurse, journalist and reporter.

Another aspect of your neurology to consider is that you may actually enjoy social situations. If you're one of these people, it might be worthwhile considering a career based on relationships, such as working with clients or students. Some of these types of jobs include being a salesperson, teacher, human resources practitioner or public relations professional.

Finally, you may look at working for yourself. If your neurology is one that enjoys excitement and risk-taking or prefers to work independently and to be allowed the freedom to be creative, this may be a suitable option to you. What you do need to consider is the day-to-day running of a business or a company, such as doing the accounts and keeping organized. If this is not a strong area for you, it may be a good idea to go into business with a partner; that way you can draw on each other's strengths in the partnership – or to hire people to help you with the tasks that you struggle with.

ACTIVITY

Write down what careers you would like to do:

....

....

Now write down what skills you can identify that you have that you think would help you to do the careers you selected:

....

....

Preparing for work

Societal expectations

As many of us know, the employment world can be a difficult one to navigate for most people, let alone for autistic/neurodivergent people. The employment journey starts way before getting a job. From a young age we are led to believe that we need to get a good education, strive for a well-paid job, earn money to buy your first car, earn more money to move out and live on your own or with a partner, save and earn to support a family, the list goes on. This is something that many people aim for, that idyllic, perfect, fulfilling life.

Barriers

But what happens if you don't fit the expectations of what society holds? What if it starts way back in the days of school where children and adolescents are being prepared to become these contributing members of society, but are struggling to navigate the education system due to differences in learning styles, being bombarded by sensory stimuli or grappling with the 'hidden' curriculum of the neurotypical world?

When leaving school, society puts high expectations on young adults about what they should be engaging in and aiming for. But again, what happens when the barriers and differences experienced through school by neurodivergent kids also affect how they perform in the workplace? It can make their aspirations, vision, goals and dreams so much harder to attain.

Transitioning from school to employment

Some questions for people supporting you to ask when you are transitioning from school to employment:

- Are you prepared and ready for the expectations of work?

- Do you know how to self-advocate and to have a voice that will be heard when you have questions to ask your potential employer, manager and co-workers?

Questions people supporting you can ask about potential employers:

- Have they been trained in and do they have a good understanding of neurodiversity?

- Are they willing to embrace and support diversity and to be inclusive of those with differences?

Where do we start?

Quite simply, our employment journey begins from the very first day we start our educational path.Parents may think that planning for their child's career from when they first start school might be a bit too young, but it is never too early to start thinking about and identifying what their child's areas of strength and interests are. Many of us autistics know from a young age what we want to do, and what we enjoy, and this often doesn't change much over time. When our parents assist us in learning about our areas of strength, what we find hard to do and barriers we may experience, it can help us define areas of learning in school that can form part of the scaffolding in working towards a job or career we may excel in and enjoy.

When we look back over our younger years, including when we first started school, we can reflect on the challenges we experienced and our strengths that helped us learn and grow throughout our school years. When we were at school, we started to identify what we enjoy doing and did well at. Our parents would have also given us guidance and encouraged us when we excelled or where passionate about an area of interest. When we reflect back, we can gather this information to help us determine what a future career pathway could look like and what support and strategies we may need to put in place along the way.

Here is an example of my (author Barb) experience of my first day of school to give you an idea why we need to start as young as possible with planning and implementing strategies that will support us through school and into work.

Case study: First day of school

Day one of school started out in a world of chaos, confusion, noise and anxiety for me. At home I had a structured daily routine with my mum and dad. I would spend endless hours in my own world drawing pictures, building with my Lego with the piles sorted into their colours and was quite content being on my own, doing my own thing quietly. Everything in my life at home had structure, until school. School was overwhelming.

The noisy kids scared me, the noisy chairs and tables tortured me, and the lighting of the room confused my vision. Standing there with my school bag, I couldn't figure where to put it on the bag racks as I needed to know exactly where my spot was, and I didn't want anyone else's bag touching mine. I was terrified and overwhelmed, and I had only been there 30 minutes. And I felt like this for many years to come.

These days, educators, family and health practitioners are recognizing autism, ADHD, dyslexia, dyspraxia and many other conditions in children earlier and even more importantly, girls and gender-diverse people that often slip through the cracks and do not get noticed until it is too late. I was one of those extremely quiet and very bright girls that was often mute, had no idea of jokes or social expectations of friends and found the library as a place of solace and a sanctuary for peace and quiet.

Also, the other kids at school just looked at me oddly or avoided me, so it was rare that I was even invited to join in to play. I just watched from the outside, wishing I knew how they knew all this stuff that I obviously missed out on learning about, that hidden curriculum of social skills.

These insights just into my own experience give us a clue as to what can and most often does happen when we transition through the school years and then into getting a job. If we don't know how to navigate this stuff early on, how on earth do we navigate it all in later life, especially when applying for jobs, attending interviews and if we are lucky enough to get a job, how do we keep it?

Things to consider before starting work

There are just so many things to think about in our earlier years that can certainly impact us in our work life. If we don't understand the social dynamics and etiquette and our own sensory sensitivities, and if we don't learn how to determine our needs and self-advocacy in school, then how do we navigate those things as an adult and understand our work colleagues, supervisors and management?

How do we understand instructions that may be vague or do the job right if we are not given the full run down? How do we even get a job if we don't have the right interpersonal skills and 'read' what the potential employer wants from us or see in us the potential we have to give to the workplace?

As you can see, there are a multitude of considerations and pre-planning over a considerable amount of our early life to set us up for success in gaining a job and having the best possible future:

Sensory considerations

Our sensory profile needs to be established as early as possible and regularly updated throughout our school years and into adulthood as our sensory sensitivities can change, or we find new ones as we try different things or be put in different environments that we haven't experienced before, and we need to document how these things may impact us.

Also, our sensory profile is likely to change over time, with some sensitivities becoming less or more intense, along with new sensitivities emerging and others remaining the same.

Sensory differences can play an enormous role in how we cope with a situation, and if we are exposed long-term to a sensory issue it may lead to overwhelm, meltdown or shutdown. We can be either hyper- or hyposensitive and gaining a better understanding of our particular sensory profile can provide insights on how to best support ourselves and knowing what supports we need in place to help us when we cannot avoid sensory overwhelm or, if we are a sensory seeker, what can we do to help us in gaining the sensory input we need in a way that is safe and does not cause disruption to other people that may be nearby.

Identifying an individual's sensory profile, focusing on the impact of sensory input and how it is reflected through behaviour is the key to success when supporting neurodivergent people in all environments – including home, school and work.

Hypersensitivity

Some examples of things which people can be hypersensitive to include bright lights and reflective surfaces that can cause mental fatigue, loud noises which can make it difficult to concentrate or can cause anxiety if the noise is unexpected, smells – for example cleaning products or perfumes can cause distress (and if you are like me with one of my major sensory issues with cleaning products, I (Barb) will actually hold my breath until I nearly pass out and try to run from the room or wave my arms frantically even if a small amount is sprayed near me).

I nearly had a major meltdown once when in an office lunchroom and one of the other co-workers started spraying disinfectant and wiping down the bench-top after making a sandwich while I was trying to heat my lunch in the microwave. The poor person didn't know what hit them as they thought they were doing the right thing by cleaning up, when in fact they had unknowingly set off my fight or flight response to the chemical smell.

This demonstrates how, as well as knowing about my aversion to chemical smells, I needed to find a way to ensure that I either wasn't in the lunchroom at the same time as other people or to let my co-workers know I had a problem with the smell and how much distress it caused me. How this is approached depends on the individual, as we all have different ways we react, respond and how we can best implement a strategy that will work for not just us, but for everyone in the workplace.

Other sensory considerations include sensitivity to being touched or touching particular surfaces. Certain fabrics can feel like wearing a cactus and labels in clothing can be really irritating.

Hyposensitivity

On the flip side of sensory processing unpleasantness is sensory-seeking. This can be problematic at times if the sensory-seeking is inappropriate. For example, in my (Barb) practice we have a child that likes to spit in their hands and rub them together as they love the slippery feel. When you have this happening in the classroom, it can make everyone go ewww, especially if the person then reaches out to touch someone after they do this. Understanding that this behaviour is also a stimming behaviour will give people supporting the child insight about how to address this. Often the seeking behaviour is also a self-soothing and calming behaviour. When someone is feeling good, it also helps them to self-regulate. So, we still want autistic people to experience the same feelings and to be able to stim and to support themselves with regulation, but we then need to think, 'OK, what can we substitute this with?'

A good substitute that can be used in the classroom and then used throughout adulthood and at work or home is a piece of satin/silky feeling material in a colour the person likes. When they are feeling the need to stim or self-regulate, they can rub their hands over the material. It could be something they carry in their pocket, or in the workplace they could put a piece of this material over their desk so they have it available at all times to touch or stroke.

As you can see, with a little thought and insight into what a person's sensory needs or aversions are, we can adapt the environment to support the person.

Room layout

Positioning within the classroom or workplace is important. Neurodivergent people often like to have the same chair, same table and same spot in class or at work. Some autistic people like to be positioned near a doorway – mentally, having an easily accessible escape route can help them feel comfortable. This is what I (Barb) do and often subconsciously, I will place myself near an exit at events so I can sneak out of the door, avoiding being caught up in the crowd as everyone gets up for a lunch break or to leave. I also try to position myself on an end row to allow me to lean away or move my chair out and away from the person next to me. I struggle here with people touching me unexpectedly, the smell of the person and if they have any annoying habits like chewing gum with their mouth open. I also have misophonia which is best explained as road rage for the ears. I am hypersensitive to people eating and certain sounds that either initiate a fight or flight response. Basically, I will feel instantly angry and upset or I will experience a vomit reaction and will want to run away as fast as I can. And the experience is immediate. This is certainly something to look into if you have sound sensitivities.

Now back to the room layout...

Some people need to be at the front of the room where they can focus on the teacher without the visual distraction of others in front of them; others prefer to be at the back of the classroom where they can't feel the eye-gaze of their peers constantly. This same layout also applies at work, especially in training or team meetings.

Changing the layout of the classroom or workspace can be distressing for neurodivergent people. This is especially true when the change happens unexpectedly. Mentally preparing for a day at work or school can require huge effort, with lots of planning, visualizing and often overthinking. Add anxiety into this and you can see how having to cope with unexpected change can really elicit a sense of losing control and be anxiety-provoking. Recovering from unexpected change is incredibly hard and the person may not be able to refocus. They might look like they are being disruptive, inflexible or zoned out – educators or employers may interpret this as someone who won't engage or is lazy.

Visual considerations

Visual sensitivities can be supported by changes in the lighting of the room. Fluorescent lighting can be painful and mentally draining for autistic people. People with light sensitivities can pick up the slight flicker cycles of the lights and their brains are processing this constantly, which is extremely tiring. As you may know from your own experience, after being bombarded eight hours a day, five days a week, your brain is tired and stressed and unable to perform at its best.

Filtered natural light is optimal for most people, but not always available. If possible, employers should change fluorescent lighting to dimmable LED lights. They still have flicker frequency but are much less distressing to those with visual sensory problems. If unable to change the building lighting, employers should consider lamps for the room.

When working with computers and tablets, try to ensure the backlighting is adjustable to the surroundings. The employer should show how to change the lighting to what is suitable to the autistic person. If a person has dyslexia, reading or tracking problems, employers can consider changing the colour theme of the program that is being used. For example, Microsoft Word has a bright white background with black text. If a person is working on this type of platform for many hours, it can be distressing in the terms of light intensity and also reading can become difficult. In my (Barb) experience, having a light blue background with dark blue text is easier to read and on the eyes in general. You can try a few options of background and text colour to see which option works best for you.

Breaking text into smaller paragraphs is easier for reading and comprehension too. If possible, have large chunks of text broken down into smaller sections, or if you are given a large piece of text, break it down first before attempting to read. You will find it a lot easier to take the information in!

Other considerations in terms of lighting include:

- Is the desk surface bright or reflective (this is where that piece of material can serve two purposes, sensory for touch and sensory for light reduction and glare)?

- Are the walls in the room visually distracting or distressing?

- Are there things like bright coloured posters on the wall?

Where possible, learn what impacts you in terms of work or learning spaces. Employers should work collaboratively with autistic employees in finding strategies and tools that support them.

Different ways of understanding

We all have different ways of learning. I (Barb) dislike eye contact, as do many autistic people. This is especially evident when I am being given instructions verbally and have to look at you. I will have no idea what you have said as I am trying to mentally concentrate on forcing myself to look you in the eye, but also finding it painful to look you in the eye. This makes it incredibly difficult to look at you and understand the words you are saying. My energy is elsewhere, not on the information you are trying to convey to me.

When I look away, I'm not being rude, it is my way of properly listening to the words you are saying so I can get a far better understanding of what you are saying. This is my way of doing my best to listen to you.

Now for me, when I just listen, I can understand the changes in the speech, can tell if there is an emotion to the words, and whether you are sincere or not. I may not be able to see the visual facial differences of emotions like many people do, but I can hear them. This shows we all have different ways of communicating and understanding each other.

The same goes if questions are ambiguous, too long or have too many requests within the question; we struggle to understand what is meant and what we are to do. I (Barb) would sometimes just stare at the floor in frustration not knowing what I was supposed to do, or nod, giving the impression I understood what they asked, but I would actually walk away highly anxious, confused and worried. I would appear incapable of what I was asked. Problem here is, we are often scared to ask for help, for fear of standing out at work or in the classroom that often has already singled us out as the 'weird one' to our peers or co-workers. We don't need any more attention. So, we sit and struggle in silence.

CHAPTER FIVE

Job Hunting: From Planning and Goal Setting to Getting and Starting Your New Job

Vision planning

It is never too late to visualize the future you want and plan to realize it.

Many young neurodivergent people have intense interests and passions that can give an indicator as to what you should strive for. Gaining employment around a passion you love or into a field that will use your intense interest as a skill is the most desired outcome.

When we think about what we would like to do as a career, we also need to consider what we need to do in order to achieve our dream job. Some people may think our ideas would never eventuate or be extremely limited in potential work opportunities. We may want to own a horse-riding stable or want to work as a chemist. These options are quite attainable and have a variety of offshoots in potential employment futures. With horses, for example, there are opportunities to work within an equestrian field and start out your working career by cleaning and caring for the horses, working up to becoming a horse trainer for show jumping or break in horses for riding stables. You could work in administration in these areas. When you think about how many career variations a particular intense interest could lead to, the doors to employment become a lot wider.

Where possible, it is always a good idea to consider undertaking volunteering in a career that you would like to do. This will give you an opportunity to experience what it would be like to work in this type of job and what the demands of the job are. This is a great opportunity to see if you really do want to pursue this type of career, identify what potential barriers are and assist in further career planning, for example with further education or training.

The same vision planning can be done at any age in life. Even at 50, it is not too late to work out how to achieve a pathway to a happier and potentially more successful employment position. At 50, I (Barb) obtained my Master's degree and now work in a field I am passionate about. It really is never too late.

Once you ascertain what your passions and visions are, the next step is goal setting to work out how you will achieve this.

Post-school pathways

Autistic people are passionate about their intense interest topics and this may not change over the years at school. However, when you don't achieve the necessary grades by the end of your education, you may shut down and feel like a failure. This can be incredibly overwhelming, and you may feel like there is nothing you can do in attaining your dream job or career.

Establishing a variety of possible post-school pathways – that is, the ways we get from school to a career – is essential in helping you to keep moving forward, rather than coming to a stop and shutting down.

It takes a collaborative team of people in working towards your goals and visions. This can be with your parents, teachers, support workers, coaches, friends; each person will play a critical part in recognizing your positive character traits and skills that can be transferable into a variety of careers and job roles.

Documenting those strengths and skills, interests and passions from everyone's point of view can provide you with a variety of options for employment and identify pathways to achieve those careers. These can:

- create a profile of your skills and strengths, interests and passions

- recognize areas you find challenging and barriers you face and develop solutions to these

- identify the way you learn

- discover possible career/job opportunities.

Goal setting

Understanding our strengths and challenges helps us to determine what we would like our goals, visions and dreams to be. Goal setting is instrumental in building self-advocacy. When we learn who we are, we can determine what we want. So, ascertaining what you would like your life to look like in the future requires some careful consideration and time to reflect on what we want, not on what other people expect. This can be done at any age.

When we are younger and still at school, we can learn with the help of parents and teachers to identify what we really like doing and how using our interests and strengths can help determine what future we would like to have. This is also applicable when we are older in re-evaluating where our life currently is, whether we are still enjoying what we do or if we haven't found what we've enjoyed doing, and taking a good look at what we can do to implement change.

For example, if you were diagnosed as autistic later in life, you may only now be realizing what your true strengths are. What has challenged you in the past will now become clear and you can learn how you can best support yourself. In the past you may not have realized that you were experiencing sensory overwhelm, due to the working environment that you were in making you stressed and anxious. You may have enjoyed doing the work but could never figure out why being at work made you feel mentally overwhelmed by the end of the day or the end of the week.

Once we start to learn about ourselves and our needs and what will help us, we can then self-advocate with those around us, explaining that by having the right supports in place, we can perform better and reduce our personal overwhelm or anxiety.

So how do we go about goal setting? What we first need to do is identify what it is that we want to work towards. We also need to work towards understanding how long this goal could take, and whether short-term goals need to be set to assist in reaching long-term goals. Often, neurodivergent people will have an idea of their overall goal, so from this vision, the best way to understanding how to achieve this is to work backwards from this large-scale goal.

When working backwards from this large-scale goal, breaking it down into smaller more achievable goals, we also learn to identify what challenges we may need to overcome and where identifying our strengths can help us with determining what supports, tools or strategies we may need to put in place to help us get to our long-term goal.

Goal setting can be a very powerful process in helping us

motivate ourselves into turning our visions into a reality. We can ask ourselves what do we want to achieve once we reach that goal. For example, let's say we achieve gaining that dream job. Is this long-term goal of working towards the job that we want also part of a bigger picture of earning a good income so we can buy that nice car or buy a place of our own to live in? By planning and identifying these key points, we are not only improving and growing our self-advocacy and self-determination, we are also working towards a more independent life.

Ascertaining strengths

Autistic people may have a natural gift for numbers, systemizing, scheduling and organizing. Others may have skills in literature and writing. Neurodivergent adults, especially those who have been diagnosed later in life, will not have had supports put in place and may feel like they will never get a job or feel they have no gifts or talents to offer. But if we take the time to plan, we can usually find out what area of interest a person gravitates towards.

Even in the most negative of situations, there is always a solution. We just need patience to find it. One example of how an apparent negative mindset can be turned into a positive outcome is a person who appears overly critical of the world around them and finds fault in everything. But their anger doesn't have to be viewed as a negative trait. A person who is angry has a fire within. They have passion and that passion just needs to be redirected. With guidance, the person with the critical mindset could potentially become a critical reviewer. Taking the time to ask them how they would find solutions to faults usually elicits an amazingly detailed and solution-focused answer. We just need to take the time to understand the person and how to turn what appear to be challenges into strengths.

Creating an instructional plan

Now that we have worked out what our support needs are, whatever stage of life we are at, we need to make an instructional plan of how to go about tackling any barriers and to review them regularly, especially at school and in the workplace.

Constant evaluation helps you, your family, your teacher and/or employer understand how you are progressing. For example, do adjustments need to be made or does there need to be another pathway taken to achieve the final desired outcome?

Workplace support plan

Following is an example of a workplace support plan for an autistic person that has a job but is experiencing some challenges. This plan is a great way to identify how to support someone and how the workplace can rethink how they can provide accommodations with the employee. This type of support plan can be used in a variety of settings, such as at school or at home, to identify potential barriers and how to collaboratively find solutions and strategies that you – or the people supporting you – can put in place throughout your life.

The table below shows workplace supports for both the employer and employee and what they can both do to work together in creating a more inclusive and supportive environment, as well as giving the employee tools to help them to support themselves at work.

	Workplace	Employee
Workplace supports	• Clear and precise instructions for what is expected with each job from employer/supervisor. • No sudden changes to roster or workplace environment. If an urgent change is unavoidable, discuss with employee how to implement unexpected change, with detailed instruction and desired outcomes. • Provide verbal and/or written instruction when employee is unclear about what is required. • Provide clarification when employee is not clear on a task. This needs to be in a calm and supporting manner to help reduce their anxiety about a situation they may not understand. • Keep task requirements to one or two instructions at a time verbally. If multiple instructions are required, if possible, provide written instruction to employee. Encourage employee to take notes of what tasks they need to do. Note-taking can be written, typed or recorded on phone for clarification and to refer back to as they complete each requested task. • If possible, have one or two specific people in the workplace that employee can communicate with directly about concerns and support needs. Outline how employee is best to contact them, when they are available and advise employee of what to expect in terms of timeframe for responding. If the person is unable to respond within specified time, provide employee with regular updates and expectations.	• Ask employer/supervisor if unclear about a situation. • Request written instruction when unclear and ask for details of what is required and outcomes expected. • Request processing time to fully understand what is expected for a task (e.g., request 10 minutes in a quiet space to process instruction and write down any concerns you have, or if not clear, what is expected of the task and ask the employer to clarify). • Executive functioning – when employer/supervisor gives multiple tasks or instructions, request them to provide you with a clear written instruction of what is needed. Or notify the person that you need to write down or record the instructions to help you follow out the task correctly. • Task inertia – ask the employer which task they want you to do first. If multiple tasks, ask the employer to outline the order of tasks you need to undertake. • Use Google Calendar as a means to remind yourself of what upcoming tasks and scheduled jobs you need to complete by a certain date.

	Workplace	Employee
Workplace meetings and conflict resolution	• Reasonable amount of notice to be given for meetings to allow for employee to access a support person if they need one. • Supply employee with an outline of what to expect in the upcoming meeting. This will help them to understand what to expect and what will be discussed. • Agenda of meeting needs to adhere to what has been outlined to employee prior to the meeting. Unexpected changes to what will be discussed can add to their anxiety. • Meetings to be conducted in a calm and understanding manner. Raised or intense voices can make employee feel intimidated. • Advise employee prior to meeting who will be attending the meeting. If there is a change to who will be attending the meeting, reasonable amount of time and notification needs to be implemented to allow for employee to prepare mentally for who they will be speaking to. • If employee is feeling overwhelmed by the meeting, time should be allowed for them to take a break and to recoup or, if not possible, to reschedule another follow-up meeting.	• To have a support person/advocate with you in meetings to help convey and support your understanding and concerns about the situation when necessary. • To request in writing all concerns with clear explanation as to reasons. • Request an agenda for the upcoming meeting. • Pre-plan for meetings with notes for questions to be raised and concerns you may have. • If you are feeling overwhelmed by the meeting, to request that meeting to be rescheduled or to take time out to regroup.

Self-advocacy	• Understand your rights and responsibilities at work. Familiarize yourself with workplace policies and procedures. • Explain your needs and ask for supports in the workplace. • Speak up for yourself in a calm and respectful manner.
Self-care	• Prepare for stressful situations with anxiety reducing strategies. For example, mindfulness using the Smiling Mind app. • Ensure you are getting enough sleep and are eating well. • Get regular exercise to help reduce anxiety and depression.

Applying for jobs

Once you have identified your strengths, interests and visions, putting this all together will help you in defining what type of jobs to apply for and how to best 'promote' your strengths to a potential employer through the application process.

Learning about the potential employer is a must when applying for jobs. Take the time to understand what the working environment is like, if there are sensory problems that could affect your ability to work effectively and whether the employer understands and encourages diversity in the workplace and is willing to support your sensory needs.

Doing your research is paramount and will also save on heartache if the job or employer does not support or encourage your wellbeing at work and your ability to do your job well. There is nothing worse than ending up in a job and environment that drains your wellbeing. As we know, many neurodivergent people have struggled and faced barriers most of their lives, so working in an environment that will support you and encourage you is a must.

What is a resume and why is it important?

Creating a quality resume is critical when applying for work. Often, many employers receive hundreds and maybe thousands of applications from jobseekers and they will be quickly scanning through these resumes in the hope that ideal candidates will stand out to them.

However, if your application stands out to the potential employer due to spelling mistakes or poor structure, the resume may not be looked at again and discarded.

When creating your resume, there are different things to consider such as:

- What information do I list?

- How much information do I give?

- Is the information I put on my resume relevant to the potential employer?

Gathering information for your resume

Getting information together about yourself, knowing what your qualities, strengths and skills are, can seem like a very daunting task. What you may perceive about yourself may differ from what other people, such as family and long-term friends, see you do and know about you, especially if they have known you a long time.

These people can be a real asset in helping you learn more about your skills from an outsider's perspective. They may see something you do really well, for example, organizing the family roster of chores, but your own perception may differ and you may disregard a skill that could be essential in a future job role, for example, organizing your work tasks for the day or week. Organizational skills are a really big asset in the workplace, so make sure you highlight this type of quality.

ACTIVITY

Ask three people – these can be family, friends, teachers, group leaders or people you have had previous work experience with – what they think you are good at. Get them to list three things each, and then compare what they have said about you. You will most likely find there is an overlap in what they say, and if all three people say the same thing, then this is a really good indicator that you have a strong skill in this area.

Write down what each person says below:

Person #1

....

....

....

....

....

....

Person #2

....

....

....

....

....

....

Person #3

....

....

. . . .

. . . .

. . . .

. . . .

ACTIVITY
Personality qualities checklist

Identifying your personality qualities can be difficult, especially when someone asks you without having the time to
consider them. Below is a list of positive characteristics
to help you identify what resonates with you. Circle the
qualities that describe you below. Also, ask trusted family
and friends to also help you to identify your positive qualities too, as this again can give you another perspective
of how you appear to other people around you.

Adventurous	Candid	Cool-headed
Ambitious	Capable	Cooperative
Analytical	Careful	Courageous
Articulate	Cheerful	Courteous
Artistic	Compassionate	Creative
Assertive	Competent	Critical
Attentive	Confident	Curious
Balanced	Considerate	Dependable

Determined	Inventive	Rational
Devoted	Keen	Realistic
Direct	Kind	Reassuring
Discerning	Loyal	Reliable
Easy-going	Methodical	Reserved
Efficient	Meticulous	Resourceful
Empathic	Mischievous	Respectful
Energetic	Modest	Responsible
Enthusiastic	Motivated	Self-assured
Even-tempered	Neat	Sensible
Fair	Orderly	Sensitive
Forgiving	Outgoing	Serious
Frank	Passionate	Sharp
Friendly	Patient	Shrewd
Funny	Persevering	Sincere
Generous	Persistent	Smart
Gentle	Plain-speaking	Sophisticated
Helpful	Polite	Spirited
Honest	Positive	Steady
Imaginative	Practical	Studious
Independent	Proud	Subtle
Industrious	Punctual	Sympathetic
Inspiring	Quick-witted	Tactful
Intelligent	Quiet	Thoughtful

Tidy	Vigilant	Willing
Tolerant	Warm-hearted	Wise
Trusting	Well-intentioned	Zealous
Versatile	Well-rounded	

How do I gain work experience?

Autistic people may find they have limited work experience. This can be due to having recently finished school or university, or they may have found it difficult finding work, especially in a career that they are interested in. It can also be difficult to apply for jobs that do not inspire you to work in that industry.

However, it can be very useful working in jobs that are not ideal, or your dream career pathway, as they can help build your skill-set, which can then be transferred to other types of jobs in the future. Examples of these jobs which build skills include customer service, administration work or learning how to conduct a stocktake of products.

You can also build your working skill-set by volunteering. There are many organizations that value dedicated volunteers and this is another great way to build your work skills and experience.

When considering volunteer work, you want to seek roles that either match your interests and passions or that will give you experience and job-ready skills that could form part of your ideal career. For example, you may need to gain customer service skills that will form part of your dream job. You could get these skills by volunteering in a café or clothing shop. These skills you acquire will then be very helpful when you apply for a role as a graphic designer, for example. Your passion may be drawing and technology, but you will also need the customer service skills to communicate with your clients to understand what they would like you to create for them and interpret that information into a design.

Many businesses and organizations are open to recruiting volunteers or interns who want to gain skills and work experience. You could email organizations asking them if they are interested in taking on a volunteer. If they say yes, then you could email them your resume or a short letter explaining what you like to do and what skills you hope to learn when working with them as a volunteer.

Do your homework on the organizations that you contact. Read through their websites, as you can gain lots of information about what their organization does. Many organizations have a page on their website that explains their vision or mission statement, and this is a snapshot of what the organization's goals are.

Same goes when applying for jobs – listing relevant skills is always a good idea; this can be especially helpful when you don't have any work experience just yet.

Even if you haven't had the opportunity to gain work experience, it doesn't mean that you don't stand a chance at getting the job. Many of us have skills that we have learned through life experiences, interests and hobbies, and these can be beneficial to a potential employer.

How to work towards my career project

When we are planning and working towards our career, it can be helpful to make a plan of what career we would like to do and how we can work towards achieving that dream job. When leaving school, we may not have the qualifications or work experience that can help us gain a role we would enjoy, so it can be helpful to look at other work options, whether they are paid or volunteer work, that can help us build our skills and confidence and can transfer into the career we are pursuing.

Below is a project for you to undertake that will help you in working towards the career you would like to do:

ACTIVITY

What career do I want to do?

. . . .

What skills are needed in this role?

. . . .

. . . .

What qualifications/training do I need to achieve my career? (e.g., TAFE, [Technical and Further Education], university, traineeship, internship, other)

. . . .

. . . .

What volunteer work could I do to help me in gaining skills towards my career?

. . . .

. . . .

What paid work could I do to help me in gaining skills towards my career? (e.g., working in a café to gain customer service and cash handling skills)

. . . .

. . . .

How many hours would I like to work?

. . . .

Do I want to work full time, part-time, casual or other?

. . . .

What is the minimum hourly wage I will get paid to do this job?

Full-time permanent	
Full-time casual	
Part-time permanent	
Part-time casual	

How much superannuation do I get paid?

. . . .

Is there a uniform I must wear or a certain dress standard required?

. . . .

What cost will be involved in getting clothing for the job?

. . . .

How will I get to and from work?

. . . .

What companies/businesses would I like to work for?

Company name	What they do	What is their vision statement? (Clue – have a look at their website)

Your resume – first impressions count

When creating your resume, there are different things to consider. Questions to ask yourself include: what information do I list, how much information do I give and is the information I put on my resume relevant to the potential employer or job.

Getting information together about yourself, knowing what your qualities, strengths and skills are, can seem like a very daunting task. It can be very useful to enlist the help of other people who know you well. People like your family and long-term friends can be a real asset in helping you to learn more about your skills from an outside perspective. What you may perceive about yourself may differ to what other people see you do and know about you, especially if they have known you a long time. They may see something you do really well, but your own perception may differ, and you may disregard a skill that could be essential in a future job role, for example, prioritizing your work tasks.

Organizational skills are a big asset in the workplace, so make sure you highlight this type of quality.

How to structure your resume

When planning out and considering what to put in your resume, the first thing that comes to mind is usually which skills you should include and what work experience you have had, especially experience that will look impressive to a potential employer.

However, while this information is important and will be critical in your landing an interview with a potential employer, you will need to know how to best structure your resume, as this can make a significant difference and be most beneficial for you.

Place your contact information at the top

Your full name and contact details should be at the top of your resume and is critical information that the potential employer will need to use to contact you if they offer you an interview.

Make sure you include the following:

- your first and last name

- under your full name have your short, approximately

25-word 'elevator pitch' (we will explore this further next)

- your address: this can be a residential and postal address

- your phone number or the best phone number to contact you on

- your email address.

Make sure to proofread these details as an incorrect phone number or email address could see you missing out on a response from a potential employer.

Elevator pitch or marketing statement

An elevator pitch is where you write just a few words to make an impact on a potential employer.

In this technological age, and with the large numbers of people applying for jobs, we need to be able to stand out from the crowd with a highly engaging sentence or two about why the employer needs us on their team.

Recruiters also benefit from being able to quickly see what your unique experiences, skills and strengths are.

Highlight your skills

Condensing your work history into 25 words or less can be challenging – it is a short, single sentence or two, so make sure you have the right information in there to catch your readers' attention. The goal is to include your most distinctive skills so that the reader is left with more knowledge and more relevant information about you.

A good example of this:

I'm a self-motivated, visual artist with five years of marketing and advertising experience, specializing in digital content with a keen interest in social media.

Ensure correct spelling and grammar

Trying to fit as much information about yourself into a punchy sentence or two can mean a lot of word juggling which may lead to grammatical errors. Make sure that your 25-word summary reads well and is easy to comprehend. Consider your tenses and make sure they're consistent. Once you have done your own spelling and grammar check, you may even want to run some options by a few friends or family to find out which one they think reads more clearly.

A good example of this:

I'm an in-house corporate solicitor with over eight years' experience, specializing in mergers and acquisitions with a focus on South-East Asia.

A bad example of this:

Gloria is an in-house corporate solicitor with over eight years' experience. I have specialized in mergers and acquisitions in South-East Asia.

Elevator pitch for students

- Name the field you are working in.

- Describe which type of company you'd like to work in.

- Name your unique selling point by stating any skills and background information that make you the best candidate.

Craft your pitch – examples

I am completing a certificate 3 in Business at TAFE. I am interested in a career in (or position as an) Office Assistant in the Accounting field. I have been involved in planning events and budgets with my local netball club.

I am completing grade 12 at high school with a focus on health and science. I am interested in a position in customer service in the hospitality field where I can use my strong planning and interpersonal skills. I have been involved in planning family events and budgets.

ACTIVITY

Complete the following elevator pitch with information about you, your qualifications and experience, and the career you are interested in working in.

I am completing a . . . . I am interested in a career in (or position as a) . . . . in the . . . . (industry). I have been involved in . . . . or have experience in . . . . or enjoy . . . . or . . . . I am . . . . (your qualities).

The elevator pitch you write for your resume will also be your opening words in an actual interview. Usually, the potential employer will ask you right at the beginning of the interview to tell them about yourself and why you would be a good fit for the job. Having a short and concise but information-packed pitch will be a great selling point about you.

This is a great way to also prepare for your actual interview and can be worthwhile practising and getting this pitch right, as it will set the tone for the interview you will have ahead.

In an interview, your pitch is usually about 30 seconds long, so you can expand on what you have written in your resume to about four to five sentences.

This is probably one of the most important parts you will have on your resume and for your interview. We highly recommend spending time on getting this put together well to reflect your qualities and strengths.

Have a strong introduction about you

This section of your resume is a short summary about yourself and your skills that needs to grab the attention of the potential employer. Keep in mind that employers will be sifting through many applications, so this statement needs to jump out and make the employer read more of your resume and to add you to their list of considerations for offering an interview. It can be difficult to know how to make your resume stand out from the crowd, so you need to find ways to make your resume eye-catching.

To start with, have an opening summary that briefly highlights your best skills and relevant experience to the job you are applying for. This is where you emphasize that you would be the ideal candidate for the job. This statement will need to be tweaked for different jobs you will apply for, but once you have your first introduction created, it becomes easier to make slight changes to suit each application, rather than creating a completely new one for each application.

Also, if this is at the top of your resume, the potential employer is more likely to read it than if you started straight into listing things like your qualifications or past job/volunteer experiences.

Tip: Read through the job description and application and identify the skills that are most important for this job. If you have these skills, make sure you list them here. You can share this with a family member or trusted friend to get their feedback.

Remember, this needs to be just a snapshot of your best qualities that will catch the eye of the potential employer.

List your skills

Listing relevant skills is always a good idea as this can be especially helpful when you don't have much or any work experience just yet. Even if you haven't had the opportunity to gain work experience, it doesn't mean that you don't stand a chance of getting the job. Many of us have skills that we have learned through life experiences, interests and hobbies and this is an opportunity to show them off, as they can be beneficial to the potential employer.

List up to 10 skills that would be relevant to the types of job you are applying for. The skills do not need to be things you have done in a paid job. They could be things related to your intense interest. In fact, your resume is a great place to demonstrate things you have gathered through pursuing your passions and how they translate into the workplace.

The skills can be software packages you have learned, creative writing skills you may have, or that you are a hard worker. But remember, you will also need to back up your claims to show how you have acquired and implemented these skills.

How you word your skills will also have an impact on the

potential employer reading your resume. Claiming that you have 'helped grow the social media following' of a page or a company you may have been doing volunteer work for will have little significance if you don't back this up with some sort of quantifiable data. So, to substantiate your claim, try to quantify how much it grew, e.g., 'the page following increased by 25%' or 'there were 750 new followers within the four weeks I was working on this project'. This can be especially helpful if you are looking at a career in marketing and sales.

Document your recent work/volunteer experience

One section of a resume that is often intimidating is the work experience section. For many people, they might just be starting out and they won't have the work experience an employer is looking for. Don't let that leave you feeling discouraged though! You should be proud of the work experience you *do* have, so show that off.

List your most recent jobs in reverse chronological order in this section of your resume. However, instead of repeating your job description like many do, use this area to your advantage. You can tell an employer what you accomplished at each of those previous jobs/work experience/volunteering, so they can see just what you're capable of. In the end, they might see this and realize just how valuable you could be to their company and give you a chance with an interview.

It's also important that you don't get too carried away here. If you've held many different jobs, you do not need to list every single one of them. An employer will not look at them all, especially if they aren't relevant to the job you're currently applying for. Keep this section short, sweet and to the point! It is best to keep your resume to a maximum of two pages. If you have more jobs than you need, select the ones which are most relevant to the job you are applying for. For example, if you are applying for a job in social media marketing then listing that you managed a social media group of 12,000 people will be more relevant than saying you worked in a fast-food restaurant.

What to include

- Companies/businesses you have previously worked for.

- Your last three employers or work experience.

- Provide the full name of the business, with the most recent first.

- The location of the business you have worked for. Just the city/town and state.

- The dates you were employed for. When you started and finished.

- The job title you had. Be precise in your title; for example, state 'social media marketing manager', rather than just 'marketing manager'. Avoid using acronyms when referring to your position, or if you need to use acronyms, write them out in full first then put in brackets the acronym afterwards.

- Document the main responsibilities your job/work experience entailed and the skills you demonstrated in the role. Where possible, use numbers or percentages to measure your success in the position.

- List any awards or recognition you may have received. This is a great opportunity to showcase your accomplishments and highlight that you excelled in this particular role or field you were working in. Awards do not need to be directly related to the job you are applying for either.

- If you do not have an extensive employment history, you can include experience that demonstrates your skills and commitment to completing tasks effectively and efficiently. This is where you can draw on volunteer experience, document if you were part of a group, club or team, how you contributed and skills required and developed, and even document how you may be responsible for organizing the family weekly schedule! These are all skills that are desirable to a potential employer.

Showcase your work: Portfolios

This can be in the form of a portfolio or website where you can provide an opportunity for the potential employer to visually see work you have done. This is particularly good to have if you are looking for work in the visual arts sector. This is also a great way to showcase your talents and skills if you have had any previous work experience.

Education and qualifications

You have worked hard to earn your qualifications, so you need to make sure you include these in your resume. As with your work/volunteer experience, you add in your educational history in reverse chronological order, displaying your most recent qualification first.

For example, you would list your certificate 3 in horticulture, then your certificate 2. If you have qualifications that are not related to each other, list the one that is most relevant to the job you are applying for first as you want the employer to see this straight up!

If you are still studying, you can add this into this section explaining that you are a current student, working towards whatever qualification. Make sure you document the qualifications you are working towards and when you expect to finish this.

Referees

List here people you feel happy with giving a character and work reference for you. These can be past employers, teachers or people who know you well outside of your family. Include their full name, their job title, where they work and a contact phone number and email address for each person. List where possible three people in the order you would like the potential employer to contact them. Good choices as referees include former managers, teachers/lecturers and managers of any volunteer work you have done. Do not include family members or friends as referees.

Proofread your resume

Imagine if an employer was going through your application and noticed a basic spelling error. Or maybe they came across a huge block of text that was meant to be split into two separate paragraphs. Immediately, they will be put off by mistakes that could have been solved in less than ten seconds with a proofread and a spellcheck. Even though it might be a chore, always check your resume multiple times before sending it.

Job applications

How to identify key words and add them to your resume

When applying for a job application, copy and paste the job description that is advertised into an empty Word document.

Depending what works best for you, print out the document or view it on the computer. Then go through the document and highlight the key words that you think the employer is looking for. The words that you highlight will give you an idea of what you need to include in your resume for this particular application.

Match, where you can, examples of your skills, work and volunteer experience, education and training, along with your personal qualities and areas that you excel in, to the keywords that you have highlighted.

Once you have identified the qualities you have that match the criteria, add these into your application.

Job advertisement examples
Graphic Designer
Job description

We are looking for a creative graphic designer with excellent proficiency in Adobe Photoshop and up-to-date knowledge to interpret our client's needs and to design solutions with high visual impact.

Responsibilities

- Design compelling and consistent digital and print creatives with the marketing team.

- Work on logo designing, promotional campaigns,

illustrations, brochures, pamphlets, print ads, and much more.

- Adhere to brand guidelines and complete projects according to the deadline.

- Coordinate with outside agencies, art services, web designers, marketing, printers and colleagues as necessary.

- Amend and format existing images using Adobe Photoshop.

- Drive online engagement with social media design trends.

- Improve the existing ad creatives and other designs.

- Work both independently and in cooperation with the team.

- Review final layouts and suggest improvements when necessary.

Dog Walking

Australia's biggest dog walking service is currently looking for a professional dog walker for their Inner West franchise!

We are currently looking for a casual walker to assist with the dogs Monday to Friday each week.

Ideally would suit someone who is flexible as hours may vary some days, but would need to be available Monday to Friday, between 8am–4pm.

Our company focuses on group walks of up to four

dogs at a time in off-leash areas. The role requires you to work independently in a company van, driving around picking up groups of dogs from their homes, exercising them and supervising their play and socialization at the dog park, before getting back in the van and dropping them home again.

The ideal candidate must:

- be available Monday to Friday

- have manual driver's licence/be authorized to drive in Australia (manual van)

- have experience working with dogs or dog walking/ handling; this is strongly desired

- be hardworking, trustworthy and reliable

- absolutely LOVE dogs or this role is not for you!

All ads accessed from seek.com and indeed.com (modified to assist with instruction/learning).

How do I know if I want to work in this job?

A great way to find out if you would like to work in a particular role or for a particular business is to do your research and find out as much as possible about what is expected of you and what the working conditions will be like.

To find out more about the business, check to see if they have a website. You can read through their website and gain useful information on what their business target, product or services are, as well as what the company's vision and mission are.

If they are on social media, this can be a really helpful way of getting a more personalized snapshot of what the business and services they offer are like. Plus, there is the added bonus of being able to read what the comments are from people who interact with their accounts.

However, if you are applying for a job that is for a small local business, for example a fish and chip shop or café, you may not be able to find as much information about them on the internet. But you can still do your homework and find out what a shop or café is like by visiting them in person.

Let's take the example of a junior position being available at the local fish and chip shop and they are wanting someone to work Friday and Saturday nights. You could go to this business during the hours they are advertising the position for as a patron. This will give you the opportunity to buy some chips from them and if possible, sit there to eat your chips and observe how the workplace runs during that time.

You can gather some good insights while observing. Make a note of:

- Smells. Are there overwhelming smells that you would find difficult to tolerate while working?

- Noise. Is the workplace noisy? Are there lots of people talking? Are there lots of instructions being given to the people working there and how easy is it to hear them?

- What is the temperature like? Do the employees look hot and sweaty?

- Textures. How would you feel about handling wet fish or slippery squid?

- Pace. Is the workplace fast-paced and staff rushing around?

- When placing your order, make note of how they take orders and payments. What is their system for processing orders?

- What is the overall feel of the business? Is it inviting and friendly? How do staff interact with each other?

As you can see, you can learn quite a lot when you investigate a potential job and the workplace!

And remember, our first jobs may not be the job we want to do as a career, but they can be a very useful stepping-stone in gaining skills and confidence that we can take with us as we work towards that dream job.

Interview process

Once you have become successful with your job application, what is probably the most daunting part now awaits: the interview. I (Barb) must say I don't think anyone who has attended an interview has not been anxious and overwhelmed at trying to anticipate what the potential employer may ask during the interview.

The best way to approach an interview is to be as prepared as possible. To start with, learn as much as you can about the workplace in the terms of what they do, what service or produce they provide and then ask yourself, how can I be an asset to this company, what skills do I bring? Write or type all these points down and take them with you to the interview.

You are allowed to take notebooks or an iPad with you and this will show the potential employer that you are actively learning about their business and bringing forward to them your strengths. You can say to the interviewer that you need to refer to your notes as you don't want to leave out essential points and skills you wish them to know about.

Often in the interview you will get asked what your strengths and challenges are. You need to be honest and only draw on the strengths that are appropriate to the job. For example, if your special interest is Star Wars, you don't want to convey that your strength is in knowing everything about Star Wars, but you can convey that you are excellent at researching and understanding a subject or product which could be viewed as an asset to the potential employer. Knowing everything about the product and how it can be used is an enormous advantage.

Often autistic people may not recognize our own strengths, so working together with a parent, teacher, partner (if you have one) or friend who knows you well will help ascertain your strengths and how these could be useful in a job.

On the flip side, don't pretend that there are no challenges. We all have them. You may think that conveying your challenges to the employer will surely be viewed negatively. No, not at all. If you are honest and upfront, they will certainly respect this, especially if you explain your challenges along with the strategies and tools you have in place that support you with this.

For example, you can convey that you struggle with details or complex tasks that are spoken to you all at once. You can elaborate by saying how you manage this, for example, by taking notes, either written or recorded so you can then break the task down into smaller parts and then schedule these parts to help you keep on task and on time. Now, you see, this is innovative thinking and shows the potential employer you are being active in doing your job well. The challenge looks more like a strength when conveyed like this.

Often at the end of the interview you will be asked if you have a question for the panel. It pays to have one prepared.

Helpful questions include asking what you will do in the role, questions about the business or what opportunities for training and development there are.

Anxiety

In my (Barb) experience, I have encountered a common theme of anxiety when applying for jobs, understanding how to fill out application forms, how to 'perform' in the interview and, if successful, what is expected of you in the workplace. Those who are employed express fear of asking for support at work, or not knowing how to ask for it.

Effective communication also poses a significant barrier for many of us autistic people; this can involve difficulty in conveying not just our needs and concerns, but also our worth and value. This barrier of effective communication adds to our anxiety and begs the question, does anxiety increase communication problems, or do the communication barriers increase the levels of anxiety?

It is assumed that providing supports and interventions prior to starting on looking for employment will help improve how we communicate our worth and skills when filling out job applications and during the interview process. Plus, depending on the supports or strategies we use, this can also reduce our anxiety levels. When we reduce our anxiety levels, it can have a wider effect on our overall wellbeing and help us to feel less stressed in social situations.

Now one support strategy that I have found effective in helping reduce anxiety is by having a mentor or a person with life experience who is also neurodivergent. Research by

Cheak-Zamora, Teti and First in 2015[1] identified that young autistic adults have limited input in how they want their future to be, with the primary caregiver or parent being responsible for most decisions about what their support needs are, and what support services they should attend. These young adults feel they have no control over their personal future and fear what is ahead for them. Without having input into their own lives, it can make them feel helpless and anxious and not in control of how their future should evolve.

Having a mentor, especially someone who is also autistic/neurodivergent, opens up the opportunity for you to have someone to talk to who is just like you. I personally have found this enormously helpful after receiving my diagnosis and connecting with people who are just like me and those people becoming my tribe.

I don't fear what I say to them and can be completely honest about how I feel as they understand me and get me as they often have similar lived experiences. This is what mentors do. They allow the person to speak about concerns openly and help them to find solutions and strategies that will work for them. If you do consider a mentor, make sure again you do your research; ask them how many people they have supported, what were the outcomes and how many have they helped in the area of gaining employment.

Another strategy that can be helpful is implementing a mindfulness routine into daily life. I want to stress here that this is not for everyone – especially if the person has a background with

---

1   Cheak-Zamora, N., Teti, M. and First, J. (2015) '"Transitions are scary for our kids, and they're scary for us": family member and youth perspectives on the challenges of transitioning to adulthood with autism.' *Journal of Applied Research In Intellectual Disabilities* 28(6), 548–560.

complex trauma, mindfulness may bring up trauma events which need to be supported in a clinical setting.

Mindfulness apps can be really helpful, especially if you use them say an hour prior to filling out an application form or attending an interview. This can help reduce the anxiety. Also, you can listen privately with headphones when travelling on public transport without drawing attention to yourself, or during a lunch break to help you reduce your anxiety. This tool can effectively be implemented anywhere, at any time, and discreetly. Plus, it is cheap to implement.

Having a smartwatch can also be useful for monitoring heart rate and being able to identify when elevated heart rate occurs along with anxiety.

Another tool that is useful in reducing anxiety is art or art therapy. Recent research identified that young people who implemented art into their routine found it reduced anxiety, especially around academic areas. It also identified that younger people have less resilience to anxiety than older people who have built this resilience up due to experience and having strategies in place.[2]

I firmly believe that working on reducing anxiety will greatly benefit neurodivergent people and will help them in many aspects of their life.

Preparing for work

What happens once you have got the job?

---

2   Karkou, V., Sajnani, N., Orkibi, H., Groarke, J. M., Czamanski-Cohen, J., Panero, M.E., Drake, J., Jola, C. and Baker, F.A. (2022). 'Editorial: The psychological and physiological benefits of the arts.' *Frontiers in Psychology* 13, 840089.

There are some things to consider when transitioning into work, especially when it is your first job, and these include how the workplace can effectively support you.

Supports in the workplace

What can employers and co-workers do to support you in the workplace?

- Give clear instructions.

- Give you tools to be successful at completing the task (e.g., checklists, daily and weekly timetables, highlighting deadlines).

- Provide training for diplomatic discussions.

- Provide education about how to respect co-workers.

- Give clear instruction about what constitutes workplace harassment or sexual harassment, what your responsibilities are around this and what to do should it occur.

- Encourage and support you to communicate.

- Value different approaches to tackling tasks.

- Value specific knowledge and put it to use.

- Earn your trust.

- Set you up for success.

You can talk to your manager when you start work about what you need at work.

Disclosure

Disclosure in the context of work relates to the decision to share your autism and any other diagnoses you may have with your manager and/or colleagues. The decision as to whether to disclose is entirely up to you. It is very rare that you would be required to disclose your autism in the workplace, so you do have the option of not doing so.

There are pros and cons around disclosure. The pros include that you do not need to keep your autism a secret at work. This makes life much less stressful. Another pro is that you can be honest, and your manager and colleagues will understand why you are a bit quirky or different. While no autistic person wants to have a meltdown at work – and for good reason – if you do and you have disclosed then things will go a lot easier for you if your manager and team know you are autistic! Disclosure enables you to connect with fellow neurodivergent and autistic folk at work. I (author Yenn) have always been 'out' as autistic at work. I am also out with my schizophrenia. People say it is brave, but I figure it is just easier than trying to keep all that to myself!

There are some cons around disclosure. Most of these revolve around people being discriminatory and ableist. Some autistic people worry they will miss out on promotions and career advancement if they disclose and there is some evidence to support that, this is in fact the case.

With disclosure, having a strategy is a good approach. Decide whether you want to disclose, what you want to say, at what point in the employment process do you want to say it and who you want to say it to. Your strategy may be different for each job you apply for/have but it is good to have the strategy each time, even if you end up doing something different to what you have planned.

Intense interests and uncommon skills

As part of our passionate interests, autistic people often have specialized skills which others don't. We may be interested in something very specific which most people do not have an interest in. This can mean that we possess skills which are very sought after. One of the authors of this book has a passion for autism advocacy. This means they are knowledgeable in some areas which others do not have any experience of in terms of their knowledge of autism.

It can be possible to translate your specialized skills into a career. Autistic interests can be varied, but they are quite often in areas that neurotypical folks do not have a passion for. This means the skills we have gained through pursuing our interests are in demand and there may be few – or no – others who have skills in this area. Autistic employees or business owners who use the skills gathered from their intense interest and translate this to their work can be extremely proficient at their chosen career. The lovely thing about using your passions as the basis of skills for a career is that you get to pursue your passion or interest and get paid for it!

Case study: Yenn's story – following a passion for advocacy

Author Yenn has had a strong passion for autism advocacy since 2012. They are now highly sought after as a presenter and author on all things related to autism. Yenn has written 12 published books on different elements of autism and has a large following, particularly on social media. Yenn's passion came about due to their sense of social justice and wanting autistic people to be able to navigate the world well and to address disadvantage and ableism against autistic people. Yenn manages a huge workload and does the equivalent of two full-time jobs. They are almost always motivated to do this and feel engaged in their work because they are following their passion. Yenn loves their advocacy work and feels privileged to be able to do what they do in an area that they are passionate about.

Autistic strengths and employment

Autistic people are all different. Autism is definitely not 'one size fits all'. However, there are a number of attributes that autistic people tend to share and some of these are highly desirable in the contact of work and careers.

Some positive autistic attributes include:

- attention to detail

- logical approach to the world – and to life

- honesty and ethics

- a low tolerance for errors

- focus

- a sense of responsibility

- respect for diversity and difference

- an enquiring mind.

Autistic people are sometimes told we are a liability at work. People can focus only on all our apparent deficits and problems. This is not a very helpful way to understand autism and autistic people. In fact, we can be seen as having a lot to offer the world of work. Don't listen to the critical people and those who tell you that you won't succeed at work becauseoif your autism or any other attribute. Autistic people can be amazing employees and business owners too and we have a lot to offer an employer or to succeed in our own business.

Benefits of pursuing a career based on your interests

There are several reasons for basing your career on your passionate or intense interests. These include:

- Probably the most obvious reason is that you can spend your working life doing something you love.

- As with the previous point, working in the area of your passionate interest means you will be getting paid for following your passion.

- You are very likely to be great at the work if it is based on what you love.

- You get to spend your time doing something you are passionate about.

- You do not need to differentiate between time spent following your passion and your time working as they are the same thing!

- It is likely that you will have a high level or skill and expertise in your chosen topic.

- You can talk to other people about your passion.

- You can continue to learn about your passion.

- You can be a leader in your field at work.

- You will most likely get a lot of positive feedback and recognition for your work.

- Your managers and colleagues are likely to appreciate you and your knowledge.

- You can be a positive example of an autistic person in the workforce. This can help other autistic people joining the labour force and can help dispel some myths that autistic people aren't good employees.

Your passions are an asset at work

Many autistic people work in jobs that are based on their interests or skills. Autistic people often have passions that can relate to the workplace. For example, a person who loves trains could work as a train driver, or station staff or building and working on maintenance for railways. Someone who has a passion for gaming could become a game designer or have a profile on gaming platform Twitch. A person who has a passion for politics could work in the public service or as a staff member in any of a number of roles at Parliament or as a staffer for a politician. A person who loves to paint could be a graphic designer, commercial artist or work in advertising.

Some autistic people work in roles which are directly related to their passions and others work in roles which also relate to their passions, but which aren't such a neat 'fit'. Autistic people working in jobs related to their passions often absolutely love their jobs. It is likely that they will be excellent employees as they are more likely to love their job. If a person loves their job, it is more likely that they will be good at it and that they won't mind devoting a lot of effort and energy on doing it. Managers tend to be very keen to have employees who love their job. Sometimes elements of the work will be very positive while others may be a challenge – such as communicating with a difficult colleague or manager. However, for many people the pleasure gained from working in an area of interest outweighs any negatives or at least puts the difficulties into perspective.

Similar things apply to autistic people who own their own businesses. If your business relates to your passion, it is likely that you will be a very dedicated and enthusiastic business owner. Many autistic people have their own business and quite often their businesses are based on their interests. An autistic child in Australia started a very successful business making fidget toys. He was successful largely because he knew what made a satisfying fidget toy and he knew what autistic people tend to like in terms of fidget toys because he was an autistic kid himself! Running a business usually requires passion and creativity and autistic people often have a fair amount of that! If you can't find a job with an employer that allows you to follow your passion or interest, it might be worth seeing if you can turn your passion into a business opportunity.

CHAPTER SIX

Positives of Autistic Staff/ Business Owners – and Challenging Assumptions

Employing autistic people – a smart move

Autistic people have a wealth of skills and talents to offer business. Some of these skills are viewed as 'soft skills' and are valuable in every workplace. Contrary to common stereotypes and misconception, autistic people have a range of skills and attributes which help them to be extremely good employees. We discussed this briefly earlier in the book. Here is a more detailed list of some of the things autistic people can often do that can make us excellent employees:

Leadership skills

Autistic people have a great capacity to be strong and ethical leaders. Many autistic people are inherently empathetic and compassionate and have strong values and standards; these are essential skills in being a good leader in managerial and supervisory roles. With high standards held for themselves, these skills assist in creating a supportive and inclusive workplace, not just for fellow autistic employees, but for all employees.

Teamwork

It is often believed that autistic people can't work as part of a team. This is a fallacy. Many autistic people work well in a team environment when that environment is inclusive and supportive of all members. It may appear that the person is working independently, but upon closer observation, the autistic person may need a quiet environment to work effectively in and to reduce sensory stress, which will allow them to come together with the team at specific times to collaborate and to present work they have completed in an environment that was supportive of their specific needs.

Communication skills

Another misconception is that autistic people are poor communicators. Again, with the right supports and the acceptance of a variety of communication methods, autistic people can, in fact, be very effective communicators. Autistic people are inclined to support and help fellow employees who may be struggling and will reach out to them. As a high proportion of autistic people have experienced difficulties within the workplace culture, they can be an enormous asset in supporting new employees and helping navigate the workplace nuances and expectations. Having an understanding mentor within the workplace who intuitively gets you can reduce anxiety and isolation significantly.

Attention to detail

This means that we can notice things that other people cannot. We can spot mistakes and errors and we can see things that other people don't even know exist! Attention to detail is a great quality to have at work and can mean we are excellent employees.

Honesty

Autistic people are often very honest. We don't like to lie. Many of us actually can't lie! This is a quality that can make us sought after at work.

Logic

Autistic people often approach life in a very logical way. This can be unusual and can be very helpful in the workplace as it means we see things that others do not.

Passions and interests

As described throughout this book, autistic people's passions and interests can make us very good employees. If we work in an area that relates to our passions, then we will be very enthusiastic and keen to work hard.

Seeing the world differently

Autistic people often have a different view of the world. This can be a big plus in the workplace, as it means that we have a different sort of approach to our work.

Seeing patterns where other people do not

This can be a great skill in the workplace and in business.

Creativity and imagination

Autistic people are often very creative and innovative. These are qualities that employers and managers often value highly.

Understanding concepts

Autistic people can often understand concepts and ideas that other people find difficult to understand.

Ability to spot errors and mistakes

Autistic people often notice errors and mistakes that other people are unaware of. We might be great proofreaders for this reason.

Work ethic

Autistic people tend to have a very high work ethic, which is a crucial element of a dedicated and loyal employee. Autistic people make valuable long-term employees as they are dedicated to doing their job well, and when supported within the workplace to be the best they can be, they will often be the employee who will be the longest serving. Respecting the autistic employee for the value and worth they bring, along with regular communication, feedback and supports, guarantees success not just to the business, but builds a successful and meaningful future for the employee. It is a win/win for everyone.

Accommodations in the workplace

Providing and accessing accommodations within the workplace is an essential element of creating a genuinely inclusive working environment – not just for autistic employees, but for everyone. Employers must be open and dedicated to creating the best outcomes through the provision of suitable supports for all employees. Employees also must have the opportunity to effectively communicate their needs and the supports that will aid them in working effectively, as well as implement any supports, strategies and tools they have acquired that will improve their working environment. Addressing these accommodations is a two-way street, but should not be viewed as a 50:50 partnership. These supports vary dependent on the person's individual needs. For example, you may only need to have noise cancelling earphones to help you effectively work. This accommodation can be implemented by the employee, without the need of employer support. Alternatively, if the employee's desk is positioned in a problematic sensory situation (e.g., under bright lights or near a noisy staff room), it is then the responsibility of the employer to work with the employee in finding a better position or find solutions to reducing the sensory overwhelm. Essentially, open communication between employer and employee will drive positive and productive outcomes.

Opportunity to grow

With the increased understanding and embracing of neurodiversity within the workplace, inclusive practices are strengthening, allowing for a wider range of diverse thinking and creating positive growth within business. Autistic people bring a unique strength, compassion and high work ethic to the workplace that must be embraced and an environment provided for them to grow. Autistic people, when supported and given every opportunity to flourish, become dedicated and loyal employees; they are the potential compassionate and moralistic leaders of our future and can be pioneers of a new way of thinking and evolving together that benefits not just autistic people, but every person within the workplace, creating a truly inclusive work culture.

Case study: Dave makes a mistake

Dave works in project management in a government department. Shortly after they got their job, they made a mistake.

When they realized that they had made a mistake they didn't know what to do. They thought about it and realized that the best action would be to tell their manager. Dave was very anxious that their manager would be angry but they knew they needed to tell her. Dave's manager was upset about the mistake but told Dave that they had done the right thing in telling her. Dave was relieved and knew they had done the right thing. The manager said that most people would not have come forward and admitted the mistake. This is an example of how the trait of being honest can be a positive in the workplace.

ACTIVITY

Think about some things about you that might be considered a positive in the workplace and write them down.

Beyond the stereotypes of autism and employment

There are a lot of stereotypes about autism. One of the most pervasive is the idea of autistic people all having savant, 'superpower' skills and being like the character in the movie, *Rain Man*. There are many more stereotypes though. These include that we lack empathy, that we are all maths and IT geniuses, that we don't fit in with our team at work, that we are aggressive or violent and that we are incompetent at our work. Like all stereotypes, these are highly unhelpful, insulting and mostly completely incorrect.

When a manager finds out that they have an autistic staff

member they can think of all these stereotypes and worry that managing their autistic staff member will be really difficult and take up all their time. Often autistic staff members do not fit any of those stereotypes, but the perception is that we do. Managers may take on an autistic staff member as an act of charity – like they are doing the person a favour by giving them a job. This is not OK and autistic employees may find it insulting. Despite this, it is often the case that autistic people bring a huge range of skills and positives to work. Managers are often surprised!

Stereotypes are not helpful and stereotypes in the workplace can mean that people don't get the chance to have a job or if they do get a job that they are not offered the opportunity to demonstrate all their skills or advance their career. One of the best ways for employers to bust stereotypes is to actually employ an autistic person and see them do their job.

CHAPTER SEVEN

Challenges and Barriers to Employment

What can stand in the way of you getting a job?

There are several reasons that autistic people do not get jobs. Some of these reasons also apply for neurotypical people, while others are issues just for autistic or other neurodivergent people. These include:

- Difficulty with job interviews. An interview can be the sticking point for many autistic people who want to find work. They may be qualified and have the right skills for the job, but they never get the opportunity to demonstrate this because of the interview. Interviews, put simply, are not autism friendly. Autistic people often come unstuck at the interview regardless of how well they could actually do the job.

- Another challenge for autistic people gaining employment is the physical work environment. Sensory issues in particular can make some workplaces impossible for autistic people to navigate. Often the things required to address sensory issues are not difficult or expensive for employers, but employers may be reluctant to make changes, even if they are requested.

- Another barrier to employment is unwritten social rules. Autistic people can be amazing employees but may not pick up on unwritten social rules and things like 'small talk'.

- A lack of self-confidence is another barrier to employment. Many autistic people will not even apply for a job because they think they won't be able to do it or that they aren't good enough, even if this is incorrect.

- Other people's attitudes can be another barrier to employment for autistic people.

- Being tasked with inappropriate work. Sometimes autistic people have a job but they are given work which is too challenging, not challenging enough or inappropriate in other ways. This can lead to people leaving a job through stress or frustration.

- Anxiety and perfectionism. These can be a big barrier to successful employment. While perfectionism might sound like a positive attribute it can in fact be very challenging and result in people leaving jobs or not applying for a job in the first place. Perfectionism is a kind of anxiety. It relates to people worrying about mistakes and failing – something very common for autistic folks.

Managing interpersonal issues at work

Autistic people can have challenges around communicating with other people. This is not because we communicate 'badly', but because we communicate differently. Not everyone understands this though and we often find ourselves accused of being inappropriate or rude. This is also true in the workplace. A lot of the world of work is centred on our relationships with our colleagues and managers, so having some tips around managing interpersonal issues at work can be quite useful.

Some tips include:

- Be aware that everyone is different and that is OK.

- Don't worry if not all your colleagues like you. Think about the people you don't like in your own life. Then think that if you are allowed to dislike people then others should also be allowed to dislike you, provided they treat you respectfully and don't subject you to bullying and harassment. You don't have to socialize with all your colleagues outside of work if you don't want to.

- Your manager and/or colleagues knowing you are autistic can be a big plus in terms of your relationships at work, especially if you explain to your manager and colleagues what autism means for you. However, it is important to note that this will not always be the case and sometimes managers and colleagues may not respond positively to your disclosing your autism to them.

- Your work colleagues are not friends (although sometimes a colleague will become a friend). You do not need to have close relationships with colleagues or managers. You just need to be civil and respectful and follow your manager's instructions.

- Don't ever assume people won't like you or be respectful of you due to your autism. You are not a burden and you do not need somehow to be 'fixed'. Many neurotypical people get along well with autistic people. Your autism should not be seen as a negative but simply as part of what makes you who you are.

- Always be civil and respectful to your managers and colleagues at work.

Managing ableism at work

Unfortunately, ableism and discrimination at work related to you being autistic can happen. Some people hold bigoted and biased views and negative stereotypes and assumptions around a range of things, including autism. If this happens in the workplace it can make working very difficult and can impact on your mental health and wellbeing.

There are a few things that help address ableism at work. These include:

- If there is the option to at your workplace, consider joining the relevant trade union. Unions can support employees who are experiencing discrimination and harassment.

- If the problem comes from one of your colleagues, you can talk to your supervisor about what is happening and ask them to help address the issue, usually by talking to the person responsible or by providing information and training on autism to the whole team.

- If you are feeling brave you can stand up for yourself and be assertive in explaining to the person that their behaviour is inappropriate. However, this can be very difficult and may backfire. If you follow this path, it is important to be prepared and to be respectful to the person whose behaviour you are calling out. You may wish to have a support person with you for the conversation. Try not to be blaming but to come from the position of 'I' statements (e.g., 'When you said this [insert what they said] it made me feel [insert feeling]'). You may wish to run what you plan to say past a friend or family member before you have the conversation.

- Get involved in diversity and inclusion networks at your workplace if your workplace has them. Inclusion networks support staff from diverse backgrounds at work. Workplaces that have these networks often have a disability network for staff with disability or caring responsibilities. These can be really helpful and can enable you to address ableism in a bigger context than just talking about your own experience.

What if I can't work in my area of intense interest?

You may not be able to find a job in your area of interest. There might be no jobs in the field or there may be no vacancies in existing businesses. You may not be able to start a business related to your area of interest for a range of reasons, which may include not having enough money to start the business, your area of interest not lending itself to a business idea, needing expertise that you don't have or needing to employ staff but being unable to afford to. If this is the case, do not despair! You can work in a job not related to your interest and spend your free time focused on it. Not everyone gets to follow their passion at work and it is not a disaster if you can't. Also, your career will happen over many years so it may be possible to work in an area related to your passionate interest in the future. The money you make from your job can go towards following your passion. You might be able to save enough money to start a business focused on your passion if that is the approach you want to take.

CHAPTER EIGHT

Personality Traits and Types

Using These to Your Advantage

Personality types and employment

There is a test called the Myers Briggs Type Indicator. This test measures several personality and character attributes. It is used a lot by employers to understand the different characteristics and personality types of their employees. One of the main measures in the Myers Briggs is introversion and extroversion and there are some other characteristics it measures. Autistic people share characteristics with neurotypical folks in this context – it does not measure neurodiversity! There is no one autistic personality type – we are all different, just like everyone else is.

However, there are some character and personality traits which are common to many autistic people. These include:

- Introversion, meaning a person draws their energy from within themselves and not from the people around them. It is important to note that not all autistic people are introverted. Some are extroverted – meaning that they draw their energy and motivation from other people.

Case study: Zhao – extroverted autistic person

Zhao is unusual in that they are a highly extroverted autistic person. Zhao is happiest when they are amongst other people and love engaging with others, especially their autistic friends. However, they are not quite the same kind of extroverted as many neurotypical folks are. They need social downtime and can get overwhelmed socially. Autistic extroverts are often a bit different to neurotypical extroverts. There is a word called 'ambivert' which describes a person who is neither introverted nor extroverted. Zhao thinks that most of the time they are an extrovert but that they also have some introvert qualities.

- Ethics and integrity. Many autistic people are highly ethical and have a very strong sense of right and wrong and need to be ethical in all their dealings.

- Trustworthy. Many autistic people are trustworthy and will do the right thing whether someone else is looking or not!

- Honesty. Honesty is a very typical autistic personality trait. We are known for our honesty and integrity. Many autistic people cannot lie even if they want to and our natural setting is to be honest. This can result in issues where a person is perceived as blunt or rude.

- Creativity. Many autistic people are very creative – in their activities but also in their thinking. We can approach topics from a different angle to others. This can be very effective in the workplace.

- Sense of social justice. Autistic people often have a

very well-developed sense of social justice and care for people who are disadvantaged.

- Unconventional approach. Autistic people more often than not have an unconventional approach to life. We 'think outside the box'. This can be highly effective in the workplace and may lead to us being sought after as employees.

- Kindness. Autistic people are often very kind and thoughtful. This can be misinterpreted sometimes but we are frequently highly thoughtful and want the best for others.

- Empathy. Once again, autistic people can be misunderstood when it comes to our empathy but we do tend to be very empathic people. Many autistic people experience hyper-empathy where they pick up on the emotions of others and actually experience them themselves.

ACTIVITY

What are some of your personal attributes and qualities that you think might be a plus in the workplace? Why do you think this?

Working with different personalities

In the workplace you will come across a lot of different people with different personalities. Some people will be like you and you will share attributes in common. You may get along well with these people – or you may not! Any work environment involves different people with different personalities. Even if you have your own business you will need to work with different people, such as customers and suppliers. This is perfectly OK, but it pays to be aware of the fact that you will be working with different people with different personalities.

Understanding your personality

Knowing what you are like and understanding your personality is an important part of applying for jobs. Many job descriptions seek staff with particular personal attributes. This often includes qualities like:

- honesty
- integrity
- positive attitude
- self-starter
- creativity
- innovative
- team player
- reliable
- problem solving skills.

Some of these might be skills that you already have. If so, that is fantastic. But how can you determine what personal attributes you might have? This could be an area where you enlist the help of someone you trust and who has some understanding about applying for jobs. This could be a parent, support worker or friend. Ask them what attributes they think you have, particularly in relation to employment. You might be surprised with what they say! You can also reflect on your personality and attributes yourself. Points to consider include: What do you think you are good at? What is important to you? Also try to remember things others have said about your attributes and character – even if they seemed a bit silly to you!

ACTIVITY
Write down five aspects of your personality.

CHAPTER NINE

Other Strategies, Tips and Thoughts around Employment

Benefits of volunteering

Case study: Yenn's volunteer job

Author Yenn was unable to work for many years due to anxiety. To build their confidence and experience at work, Yenn took a volunteer role at a gallery. This had a number of benefits, including building Yenn's confidence and knowledge in the workplace. The volunteer job also meant that Yenn was less worried about costing their employer money – something which had resulted in significant stress in other, paid jobs. Yenn was a great volunteer and ended up adding their volunteering experience to their resume. The manager of Yenn's volunteer job in the gallery offered to be a referee for a professional job as well. Volunteering meant that the employer for the professional job thought Yenn was an excellent candidate, as most people do not donate their labour for extended periods. Volunteering was a huge positive for

Yenn and was a catalyst for them getting the professional role that uses their skills and which they enjoy.

As we have seen from Yenn's experience, volunteering is not necessarily only about giving. There are often career benefits related to being a volunteer. Some of the benefits of volunteering in a careers context include:

- Volunteering demonstrates a commitment to working, looks great on your resume and reflects well on your application for a paid role.

- Volunteering can put you in a better position to apply for a paid role in the industry where you are volunteering. It not only provides experience, but it can also expand your network of potential employers as you will meet people through your volunteer role who may become your manager.

- Volunteering is a great way of gaining experience of the workplace for people starting out in the world of work.

- Volunteering can give you contacts who can support your career (e.g., by giving you references or mentoring).

- Volunteering can involve engaging with areas of interest or passion and can be a stepping-stone to a paid role in that area.

However, there can be situations where volunteering is used by unscrupulous employers as a way of getting ongoing free labour. Volunteering should not take the place of paid work. Ideally volunteering in the context of building your work readiness should be short-term and not a replacement for a paid role. Autistic people can be taken advantage of in this area which is not OK.

Transferable skills

Skills learned from one job can be transferred into another role. Your career involves this process on a continuous basis. Skills learned now translate into different work roles and this continues throughout your entire career. Your skills do not necessarily need to be related to prior work experience. Some of the skills used in your life outside of work can transfer to the workplace. Your passions and interests – whatever the subject – come with a range of transferable skills and these can feed into your employment. Similarly, the skills you gain through being at work can translate into the skills you use in life outside of work.

Case study: Gabe – knowledge of Marvel Comics

Gabe is 22 and autistic. They have recently started a job at a shop which sells games, comics and related items. Gabe absolutely loves the Marvel universe and there is a large amount of Marvel products at the shop. Gabe has educated their colleagues about all things Marvel and is enjoying learning about the other products too. In fact, Gabe has been researching some of the other fandoms that the shop sells and is getting very enthused and passionate about these things as well. Gabe has also learned some more things about the Marvel universe from their colleagues. If any customers have questions about Marvel, they are directed to Gabe, but Gabe also wants to become an expert in the other products that the shop sells, even if their passion is Marvel.

Qualities of autistic managers

There is an assumption that autistic people cannot be managers. This is not correct. Autistic people are in all roles in all industries and at all levels. There are definitely autistic managers in the workplace. Author Yenn has had more than one autistic manager over the years in their public service career. In fact, at the moment Yenn themselves is a manager, having one staff member reporting to them and recently they had two staff, one of whom specifically asked to have Yenn as her supervisor. Just like all autistic staff do, autistic managers often have some shared attributes. These include:

- A direct style of communication. Autistic people tend to be direct communicators and managers are no exception.

- Honesty. Autistic managers are more likely to 'tell it like it is'.

- Very caring. Many autistic people are kind and thoughtful and want the best for their employees.

- Issues reading non-verbal cues. Autistic people often struggle with non-verbal communication such as facial expressions and body language.

- Different sorts of behaviour. Autistic managers may behave in ways that neurotypical employees think is unusual or strange.

- Low tolerance for errors – spotting errors and inconsistencies that others may miss.

- Seeing patterns in things that others miss.

- If the work area relates to their passions, autistic managers may be extremely engaged in the work.

- Strong work ethic. Autistic managers often have a very strong work ethic.

- Ethics and integrity. Autistic managers are often very ethical and respectful and have a strong sense of integrity.

- Rules-focused. Autistic managers are often driven by the rules and have low tolerance for rule-breaking.

Autistic staff may get along well with autistic managers. However, this is not always the case and there is no guarantee that an autistic manager and their autistic staff member will have a positive working relationship.

CHAPTER TEN

Understanding and Managing Workplace Relationships

When we start working, there are many things to consider that are outside of doing our job. When we are at work, we often have to navigate working with other people. Our managers, supervisors, team leaders, human resources and co-workers are just some of the other people we may need to work with and communicate with regularly.

Here are some of the things to consider when working with other people and what actions you can take to ensure you have a healthy working environment.

Making friends at work

It can be quite scary when starting a new job, especially when we don't know anyone that works there. This can feel a bit like the first day of school or when transitioning from primary school to high school. We can feel very anxious and worried about how to make friends and connect with other people.

When we are at work, our main priority is to do our job.

However, developing friendly relationships with our co-workers is an important part of creating a positive and healthy workplace culture. When we make friends, it can make us feel included and part of the team. Making friends can also boost our mental wellbeing, which can also assist us with our productivity at work, and may become part of our work-life balance if we decide to grow our friendships with co-workers outside of the workplace. Another positive of creating friendly relationships with our co-workers is that it can assist us in feeling less anxious about asking for help or support and reduce our fears of being judged. Many autistic people struggle with high anxiety, so having a friendly person to talk to can really make the difference to our working day!

How do we make friends at work?

If you feel comfortable, take the time to introduce yourself to some of your co-workers. This can make us feel very anxious as we often don't know how the other person will respond. The best way to do this is when your co-worker is not busy doing their work. This can be done during break and lunchtimes. If you are feeling very anxious, you may want to watch and wait until there are only one or two people in the lunchroom and introduce yourself then. Usually, the other person will tell you their name and learning, remembering and using their name can make the other person feel you are interested in them and making them feel welcome.

If you don't have an opportunity during the breaks, you may be able to introduce yourself before or after work. But remember, at these times of the day our co-workers may be focused on getting ready to start their day or are feeling tired at the end of the day and may be in a hurry to get home.

Another way we can introduce ourselves is when we work with another co-worker. This can be a great way to introduce ourselves briefly and then get on with our work. This can reduce our anxiety by not feeling we have to make small talk with another person as we often only have a very small amount of time to introduce ourselves and then get on with our work.

Once we have introduced ourselves, we can then implement daily greetings of hello and goodbye to our co-workers. We can do this over a period of a few days or weeks, until we feel confident enough to ask them a question about themselves. We could ask them about their weekend or any hobbies they may have. When we ask them a little about themselves, we are making a stronger connection with the other person. We can also share a little bit about ourselves with them too. Ideally share something about what you are interested in as this can make the conversation easier, as you know your hobbies and interests well. Remember to keep these initial conversations brief while we get to know the other person and they get to know us too.

Another way to make friendly relationships at work is to be positive. When we are positive, other people are more likely to want to be around us. And the same goes for us. We enjoy being around people that make us feel uplifted, positive and happy. Also, when we have a positive mindset, we can inspire others in the workplace to be positive too!

As friendships grow, you may find that you can foster meaningful relationships with co-workers that expand outside of the workplace. Alternatively, you may find you only want to have connections with co-workers while at work, keeping your time outside of work for you and other friendships you may have. Ultimately, workplace relationships are based on what you feel comfortable with and it is perfectly OK not to want close friendships at work.

Appropriate workplace interactions

In the workplace, respect is one of the most important inter-personal skills to have as it can create a positive workplace culture. This is particularly helpful when you are working in a team environment. A respectful attitude should be practised by all staff members and management, regardless of how you or the other person may feel about the other person. If we do not get on or 'gel' with another person in the workplace, it is still always important to give the other person respect when we are doing our workplace duties.

A respectful attitude entails giving co-workers or manage-ment your full attention, listening to their opinions (even if you do not agree with them) and speaking politely to the other person. When we adopt a respectful attitude, it can help us understand more about the other person and their views and choices, even if they differ from ours, and it can also reduce the incidence of conflict when we take a calm and respectful approach when a problem arises in the workplace.

Respect in the workplace can reduce stress and have a pos-itive effect on our mental health. When we are less stressed, we feel more comfortable in sharing our opinions and ideas. Respect can also improve workplace satisfaction, especially when working together in a team environment and respecting different views and opinions. It also allows us to potentially learn new skills or to take a different view on a project or task you have been assigned to do.

Most importantly, respect creates a fair working environment. Respect from management allows for employees to demonstrate their skills and knowledge, giving everyone in the workplace a chance to have their voice heard. Each employee's voice is valua-ble regardless of where they have come from, their background, their culture or their neurological difference. When we are given fair and respectful opportunities, it allows for everyone to be heard. This is incredibly powerful, and as an employee, this can assist you in advocating for yourself and your opinions. When we are respectful, we can thrive in the workplace along with our co-workers.

How to show respect at work

Listen to the other person

When we take the time to listen, we are giving respect by allowing the other person to convey their thoughts and opinions. Even when we feel eager to share our thoughts and ideas, it is always good practice to allow other people to have their say without being interrupted. Plus, it is always good to check with everyone in the room if they have had their opportunity to speak. When you check in with everyone and encourage others to contribute, it is being fair and respectful.

Acknowledge the accomplishments and ideas of others

In the same way we respect other people by listening and sharing their opinions, we can also show our respect by praising or acknowledging good ideas from co-workers present. This is a great way to build positive connections with your co-workers and it can also build confidence and self-esteem for the other person. You never know, your co-worker may be feeling anxious or unsure of themselves, so a positive comment from you could make all the difference!

Demonstrate trust

People feel respected when they feel they can trust you with information they share with you. If a co-workers share sensitive information with you, take this as an act of trust from them to you and respect the person by not sharing the information with other people. If you are unsure if you can talk about information you have discussed with a co-worker or management, it is always best to ask them first if you can share this information or discuss it with other people.

Help your co-workers

Everyone makes mistakes. We can show respect when we assist the other person by politely explaining what the issue or problem was and then offer to show them how they could do this the right way or a different way. Where possible, giving the other person encouragement and productive input will help build their worth and self-esteem.

Be aware of your words and actions

When we take the time to check in with ourselves, how we are reacting to the other person can help us gain better insight on how other people may view us. If we are stressed or over-whelmed, we may come across to the other person as blunt, annoyed or angry. When we check in regularly on how we are feeling, it can help us to decide if we need to take a break, implement some self-care practices, such as putting on headphones if the room is noisy or stepping away from the computer screen if we have been looking at it too long, before we interact with other people. Just taking five minutes for yourself can make all the difference when you do finally talk to another person.

Make common courtesy and politeness your daily habit

When we are polite, other people are more willing to help us or work with us. Adding in a hello in the morning to your co-workers as you start the day, or a please or thank-you, can have a significant impact. Taking the simple steps of incorporating polite language in your day will go a very long way!

As we can see, understanding how to be respectful to our co-workers and management can bring a healthy and positive working environment. The tips we have just covered also apply to you from your co-workers and management. The respect you give to them should always be reciprocated to you.

Other things to consider when working with other people

Accept criticism

It's hard to accept criticism, especially if you have perfectionist tendencies. But, in reality, none of us are perfect and we all make mistakes at times. Yet constructive criticism is essential in order to progress and grow at work.

When you're presented with an opposing view, don't jump on the defensive straight away and try not to become distressed. Be calm and thoughtful. Take time to think about what is being suggested and whether it, in fact, is a better solution. Mistakes do happen and do not mean you are incompetent, nor are they a reflection of your intelligence.

Try to rectify the mistake or problem if possible or ask for some guidance and advice on how the situation can be avoided in the future. It is a good idea to own up if you make a mistake too. Hiding or covering up is not a good idea and, in the end, you will be better off telling your manager about the mistake when you notice it.

Socialize in new settings

Placing ourselves in social environments that we usually wouldn't be in can help build confidence levels. The more accustomed we become to different experiences, situations or environments, the easier it will become to navigate these situations and to also determine how long we want to attend these social situations for, or to determine if a situation is not for you.

So how can we ease ourselves into participating in workplace social situations?

We can consider our intense interest as a starting point. There may be the possibility of joining a local group that is based around your interest. This can be an opportune way to learn and expose yourself to social situations in an environment that is based around something that you are interested in. When we are interested in something, it helps us as we have knowledge and information that we can convey to other people within the group. This information can be helpful to other members and be valued by them as well. This can also provide a sense of belonging to the group.

This will also help you to feel valued and help grow your confidence around a group of people based around an intense interest. Also, within these types of groups, once you have been there for a short while, you can test out skills that you may wish to improve on or acquire, which you can then use in the workplace.

A good example of a skill that you may wish to test out is public speaking. You may want to improve your public speaking skills and you can do this around your intense interest within a group that is also highly interested in your topic. This will help you build confidence through presenting and speaking to the group and the group can encourage you by giving you feedback on the presentation that you delivered.

Joining interest groups outside of the workplace will allow for you to make connections and friends with people that are not reliant on your experiences through the workplace. If you are in the workplace where you are finding it difficult to make friends, or feel that you cannot connect with any of the people in the workplace due to them having very different interests and pursuits to you, having this outside group will give you that much-needed friendship and support when you are out of the workplace, and can help you get through the working day by knowing you have a circle of friends that you will be meeting up with later.

Often autistic people can feel isolated and alone, so finding a group of people through intense interests can potentially reduce that feeling of isolation and loneliness and can also help you get through a mundane day at work. Having something to look forward to when you finish work is also a good motivating factor.

Take on a challenge

When you are in a group of people that you feel comfortable with, it can provide opportunities for trying something different or taking on a challenge to push yourself to do something that you have often felt anxious or scared to do. So, with the example of public speaking, practising this with a group that you feel comfortable with will help you to transfer those skills into the workplace.

The presentation skills that you gain from outside groups can be transferred into holding a presentation for the workplace. It may also be a critical skill in helping you gain a promotion or moving up the ladder in the workplace. When we practise challenging ourselves in safe situations, this will help us to feel less anxious and to actively take on a task or put ourselves in a situation that we might not usually do without this external practice and experience.

What often hinders us in growing our skill-set is the fear of failure or doing it wrong. This can render us unable to do it due to severe anxiety about trying something new. Also, if we have had previous unpleasant or negative experiences, these experiences can impact on how we will feel about trying a new task or taking on a new challenge, due to reflecting on the outcomes from these previous negative experiences and attributing them to what may happen if you try doing something new.

Ideally, in the workplace, supervisors and managers can help build our confidence in trying new things by giving us regular constructive feedback. This information is valuable to us and will help us try new things when we are supported and receiving regular feedback on how we are going. This also contributes to growing our sense of self-worth and self-esteem.

Remain positive

Having a positive attitude at work is essential in creating a healthy workplace. When we are with people who are pessimistic, negative, or who are constantly criticizing a co-worker or management, it can become quite tiresome and overwhelming.

It can be incredibly difficult for us to be positive within the workplace when we are highly anxious and fearful of failing or not understanding what is expected of us.

This is where a whole workplace approach is necessary in supporting us to feel valued and included with the workplace. When workplaces make a concerted effort in supporting autistic people to be the best they can be, by truly including them in the workplace by working with them to provide supports that will help them, it all adds to re-establishing their sense of self-worth and confidence. When we feel valued and better about ourselves, it can change our outlook from one of anxiety and fear to one of feeling more confident and positive that is then reflected through your work and productivity.

Identifying unhealthy workplace relationships

This next section covers unhealthy relationships in the workplace. These types of relationships do not happen very often, and healthy workplaces will not have these things happen due to making sure all employees understand inclusivity and respect for other co-workers. Alternatively, if there is a problem in the workplace, it will be addressed quickly, and appropriate support provided. However, we felt it was important to cover unhealthy and toxic workplaces to help you identify early if you are experiencing anything unpleasant within the workplace. Unfortunately, many autistic people may not see the signs early as we take people at face value and expect other people to treat us the same way as we would treat them. But we want to assure you, the following information does not reflect what to expect in the workplace and it is quite rare to experience the following unpleasant situations at work.

Toxicity in the workplace

When we are at work, we expect other people to treat us fairly and appropriately. Unfortunately, sometimes we can experience unpleasant or challenging interactions with people that can have a lasting impact on our psychological wellbeing. This can also affect our self-esteem, self-worth and self-confidence.

However, workplaces do have policies and procedures in place to tackle problematic people in the workplace. These policies and practices are there to ensure your wellbeing, safety and working environment are of the highest priority and that action will be taken swiftly if you encounter a problem in the workplace.

If you do have an unpleasant or challenging experience in the workplace, you need to consider if you're being treated unfairly or poorly so you can address the situation. This can be by talking to other co-workers, to supervisors and to the employer about the situation. This can give you other points of view on what is happening or if you are misunderstanding what the other person is doing. Often a lack of communication can lead to misunderstandings. If possible, request a meeting with your manager or supervisor to discuss what you are experiencing. Your manager will then investigate the situation to get an overall picture of what is happening and take appropriate action. This can be by having a meeting with the other person or a group meeting with yourself and the other person and the manager. Sometimes when we take the time to listen and understand both sides, a resolution can be found quite quickly. Talking openly about the problem and listening to what each person has to say can help implement changes or clear up misunderstandings.

In the rare instance that management or your employer fails to respond or act accordingly to your concern, you do have rights. Having a good understanding of the workplace and policy procedures and your rights will help you in taking the correct action when the workplace is toxic and you're not getting any resolution. I do want to emphasize that this does not happen often in the workplace, but would like to make you aware of the signs of problems in the workplace, if you are unfortunate to experience this.

Some signs of a toxic workplace include:

- bullying

- harassment

- employees are stressed and unhappy

- high rates of people leaving for other jobs

- discrimination against people from intersectional groups (e.g., disability, First Nations people, LGBTQIA+ people)

- favouritism

- managers are not approachable

- high levels of staff taking stress or mental health leave

- cliques and groups of colleagues excluding others.

As good practice, we recommend that when you first start your job, you take the time to read through the company's workplace policies and procedures manuals. These manuals will give you clear information on what is expected in the workplace and what to do if any issues arise. A good employer will have this information readily available to you and you will be given a copy when you first start your job.

Another thing to familiarize yourself with is the disability discrimination legislation in the country where you live. This legislation protects you from being discriminated against in the workplace because of your disability. It also protects you in a variety of settings outside of work as well. This can be in Education, when going to a restaurant, accessing government services and using public facilities are just some of the many things that discrimination legislation covers. Better understanding of our rights and responsibilities, and of what is fair treatment in the workplace, can help us to determine what our next steps are and to confidently advocate for ourselves.

What does unfair treatment in the workplace look like?

If your job, which is mostly very positive and inclusive, has some elements you don't like, it is best to reflect that you enjoy your job most of the time and that is a pretty good outcome. However, if you are being bullied at work or facing sexual harassment or other discrimination then that needs to be addressed. In such circumstances you can talk to your supervisor – unless they are the one doing the bullying or harassment in which case contacting their manager – if they have one – is a better approach. If your workplace has a human resources department you can raise complaints around bullying and harassment with them and if you are a member of the relevant union, you can also raise issues around bullying and harassment with them.

Bullying and toxic people

Toxic workplaces often have a culture of bullying and harassment. This sort of behaviour can be obvious, but it also can be quite subtle. Subtle bullying can present as the other person who is bullying you telling you that you are misinterpreting the situation and turning the situation back onto you. This is where your gut feelings can help you in deciphering the situation and will give you clues on identifying if this person is being unpleasant or is manipulating you, rather than you misunderstanding the situation. Our gut feelings can be very important and often are the first signs that something is not right with a situation. The sooner we act on how we are feeling in a situation, the sooner we can get to the source of the problem and take action.

Manipulation

An example of manipulation is when you feel anxious about going to work because you don't know what to expect from the employer or co-worker. The person may appear friendly, supportive and a great mentor, but at other times they act like a completely different person. They can offer to help you out but then make you feel obligated to do something for them. In other situations, they may react negatively when you share your thoughts or opinions or be dismissive of you.

Recognizing the signs of manipulation is very difficult and it is often not until quite some time later we realize we are being manipulated. We trust people and expect they will treat us the same way we treat them. Often manipulators are out to use people to build their career, to boost their ego and, most of all, to control people around them. They feel empowered by having control in the situation and taking the advantage. You may not experience these feelings at first, but over time and with reflection the patterns become obvious.

Signs that you are being manipulated
You feel depressed, fearful, anxious or sad around this person
As previously discussed, you may have a slight sense that something is not quite right but disregard the anxious feelings as nothing and continue to concede to the needs of the manipulator. It is not until quite some time later, once your self-esteem and worth have been eroded, that the realization hits that you have been manipulated and by then it can now be too late to get out of the situation or you can be fearful of saying no to this person.

You feel obligated

Obligation can be a form of manipulation, especially when the manipulator expects something in return from you, even if it makes you uncomfortable. What is worse, if you do not fulfil your obligation to this person, they have an uncanny way of making you feel guilty, even if you disagree with what they are asking of you, especially when you know it is wrong.

You change your behaviour/morals to suit the manipulator

In manipulating relationships, the person being manipulated will often change their behaviour, their moral standing and approach to work in an attempt to please the manipulator. Unfortunately, no matter how much we change to try and please the manipulator, they are never going to be satisfied. Their energy is gained by controlling you and making you feel less than them. All you will do is expend your energy and feel drained and defeated around this type of person. They are energy thieves.

The manipulator's behaviour/reactions are unpredictable

This is why it can be difficult in the early days to recognize if the person is using you or is a genuine supportive co-worker. Often in the beginning they can appear helpful, friendly and on your side, then 'Pow!', their behaviour suddenly changes, and you ask yourself, where on earth did that come from? You will question yourself as to what you did wrong, whether you missed something, leading to you becoming anxious and stressed about why the other person is angry and upset.

Usually, you have done nothing wrong. It can be due to something totally unrelated, but they will take it out on you and there is nothing you can do to prevent or stop the behaviour as it is always completely unexpected, unwanted and unacceptable.

You feel your sense of value is being lost

A manipulator will find a way to make you feel devalued. They may point out that your ideas are ridiculous or that your opinion is not wanted. They will also downplay your achievements. This can be through saying that anyone could do that, you didn't deserve the recognition or by having an attitude of 'so what, what is all the fuss about?'

I (Barb) have personally experienced this with a colleague when I attended a business event where there were lots of business people from different organizations attending. The person I was with would not actively listen to what I was saying to them, but instead they would be looking around the room scouting for more important or prominent people they could talk to, to inflate their sense of self-importance. When they found their target, they walked away mid-conversation and I was left feeling confused as to why they just walked away, inadequate as they did not invite me to join them to talk to the other person, and that I was not important enough to be there.

How do we stop manipulation?

Prevention is always the best approach, but this can be difficult as often we don't recognize we are being manipulated until it is too late. This is where we start to pull together how our body is feeling and identifying what we are feeling, for example, anxious or uneasy, and connecting those feelings to the situation and/or person we are with. We can also ask fellow co-workers or supervisors or employers if they feel there is something not quite right with the person of concern or if they are also experiencing problems with them.

If you feel you are being manipulated, document each action and interaction you have with that person. Write down how you are feeling, what is being asked of you and how they behave. By doing this you are collecting evidence of the problematic behaviour that you are experiencing, and this is incredibly helpful when making a complaint about the person to management.

We need to set strong boundaries for ourselves and stick to them, even if the other person makes you feel uncomfortable. By setting strong boundaries, you protect your own wellbeing and you make a statement that you will not tolerate this type of behaviour and manipulation.

This is where speaking with employers or management to highlight the problematic person and the issues you have experienced with them is helpful on a larger scale. When management are notified, they can actively take action and appropriate measures to ensure other employees are not subjected to, or do not continue to be subjected to, this type of behaviour.

By standing up for your worth and values and setting strong boundaries, you are taking care of your mental wellbeing, as well as being part of the change in a toxic workplace.

Saying no

Saying no can be really hard to do, but it is so important that we say no in many aspects of our lives to ensure good mental health and wellbeing!

Taking the time to build our self-advocacy skills and know what our limits and abilities are, can build our confidence in saying no a whole lot more!

When we learn to say no, we are creating healthy boundaries for ourselves, we are putting ourselves first, and we realize that we need to look after our wellbeing to ensure that we can continue working in an effective and productive way, to be a good friend or partner and to realize our limits and to say no when we cannot give of ourselves.

We need to step away from the misconception that saying no is being uncooperative, selfish or difficult.

We also need to realize that, by saying no, the consequence will not be that we will no longer be asked to take on tasks or, more concerningly, that we may lose our job if we keep saying no when we are already at capacity at work.

We may also find it difficult saying no due to the fear of not being liked or accepted as we may have experienced this during school and in many facets of our lives.

We also feel guilty when we say no, and we feel like we are letting down our employer, our work colleague or friends or family.

How do we know when to say no?

Saying no is often associated with negativity, but if we continually say yes to everything, it can lead to more problems than if we just simply say no.

It is critically important to know when to say no, and to do it before we become too overwhelmed from taking too much on.

If we keep saying yes, keep pushing ourselves to breaking point, we are setting ourselves up for failure through incomplete tasks, doing our job half-heartedly or carelessly, which can then lead to eroding our self-esteem and value. It also means that people will expect us to say yes to everything and will keep placing demands on us, even when we don't really want them to.

What we need to do is think it through.

We don't have to answer things straight away.

You can ask your employer or work colleague to give you some time to think through something they have requested of you and say you will get back to them, as you want to check your schedule and check how much work you currently have on.

We also need to ask ourselves how long something will take us to do, and to ask what the deadline is for its completion, as this can affect other jobs that you are currently doing.

When you take the time to ask yourself these questions, you can give yourself a realistic idea if you can complete this work on time and to your best ability.

Also, when you ask yourself these questions you can then analyze the situation to see if you are being stretched too far, or if other tasks are priority.

As you assess your own situation through asking these questions, it will become obvious if you can or cannot take on more work or do something for someone. And this goes for anyone. It can be family, friends or partners.

How to say no positively

So, how do we learn to say no and how can we say this in a positive way?

Depending on your preferred communication method, whether you prefer to speak directly to the person or send an email, you need to explain your current situation and why you cannot take on further work. Recognizing your best way of communication can also have an impact on how you convey your response. For example, emails can be easily misconstrued due to the perceived tone or the way that we write our responses. To us it may sound like we are being clear and direct, but to the receiver it may appear unfriendly or abrupt. We need to be careful in how we convey this information.

For example, we don't want to start out by stating how much work we already have on, how over-worked we are, and that we feel they are being inconsiderate by not understanding this or knowing just how overworked we are. This can come across in a passive-aggressive way.

What we need to consider is thanking the person for considering you for the task and then explain to them that you are unable to take on this project and give your best to the task. You can also explain to the person your current priorities and explain to them how important it is to get these done, as you are already committed to them, and want to ensure you get them done efficiently and well.

Interoception – recognizing what our gut feelings are telling us

This section will discuss interoception and how it can be beneficial to us in the workplace.

Kelly Mahler (www.kelly-mahler.com/what-is-interoception/) is the author of the book *Interoception: The Eighth Sensory System,* and she explains what is meant by the term interoception:

> Interoception is a sense that provides information about the internal condition of our body – how our body is feeling on the inside.
>
> Interoception allows us to experience many body sensations such as a growling stomach, dry mouth, tense muscles or racing heart.
>
> Awareness of these body sensations enables us to experience essential emotions such as hunger, fullness, thirst, pain, body temperature, need for the bathroom, sexual arousal, relaxation, anxiety, sadness, frustration and safety.

At the most basic level, interoception allows us to answer the question, 'how do I feel?' in any given moment.[1]

Interoception at work

Interoception is a critical part of understanding and identifying how we feel in a variety of situations. Using interoception can assist you in understanding how you feel and recognizing what is making you feel that way, in many situations. We often use interoception in helping children and young adults to identify what sensation they are feeling and to connect this sensation to the emotions they are experiencing.

We also need to be able to identify how we are feeling in a variety of situations, especially in the workplace. For example, if I feel anxious about undertaking a task that my employer or colleague has asked me to do, I can ask myself why am I feeling this way? The feelings of butterflies and nausea or dread are often associated with anxiety. This anxiety is coming from a place of fear, which could be associated with not knowing how to do the job, the fear of asking for help, the fear of not getting the job done on time, or the fear of saying no.

When we recognize how we are feeling we can act upon it. In this example it can seem quite obvious we need to ask for help. When we do this, it will reduce our anxiety and bring our bodies back into a sense of calm. The sooner we act, the less time we will feel stressed, anxious or drained.

As you can imagine if this is happening multiple times a day, we are using up our energy and depleting ourselves.

---

1   Mahler, K.J. and Craig, A.D. (2015) *Interoception: The Eighth Sensory System: Practical Solutions for Improving Self-Regulation, Self-Awareness and Social Understanding of Individuals with Autism Spectrum and Related Disorders*. Shawnee, KS: AAPC Publishing.

Gut feelings

Once we learn to recognize the more obvious feelings, we can work on identifying some of the more subtle feelings we may experience. Especially those feelings that are often termed 'gut feelings'. At times we may experience an odd feeling and we can't quite place why we are feeling it. We know that something is up, but don't know what is causing this. When we take the time to sit with the feeling and analyze the current situation in the workplace, we can start to put together what may be affecting us in this way.

It may be that you have been asked to do a task but the way it was conveyed to you didn't sound quite right. Maybe there was a change in the tone of the way the person said it to you. Picking up on these subtle cues can be essential in being able to know how you are feeling.

As previously highlighted, many autistic people are highly empathic and can sense the feelings of other people around them quite strongly. Another person may not pick up these slight changes in others, but to many autistic people, it triggers a response telling them there is something not quite right.

When we act upon these feelings, we are getting an understanding of the uncertainty. If we don't act on these feelings, they can build into anxiety and stress over a few hours or days, and we cannot figure out why we are feeling so anxious as nothing obvious has immediately happened that we can link this now overwhelming feeling to. Those subtle feelings can get suppressed or lost during the day, but they do stay with you, adding to mental stress.

What we can do in situations like this is act immediately. If the person is sounding indifferent, then ask them if they are feeling OK. Often it only takes something small, like asking if the person is OK, to find the reason they are feeling this. If you are sensing hostility, anger or irritability in the tone, you can ask the person, 'Is there a problem with this job as you seem somewhat tense? Is there anything I can do to help here?' If you don't feel safe in asking the person, you can act by speaking to a colleague, supervisor or employer to see if there is anything wrong and if there is anything you can do. By asking, we are seeking clarity which can reduce our internal feelings.

Sometimes the answers we get may seem quite negative, but all communication is creating a starting point to resolve the situation. The sooner we can identify the problem the sooner we can put our anxiety and stress to rest.

Some practical strategies and considerations at work

There are several things you can do to help you do your job well and thrive at work. Some of them are listed below.

- If your workplace has one, you could get involved with the Disability Network (it might be called something different to that, such as 'Ability Network', etc.).

- Find a mentor. Mentors are people who provide leadership and guidance to others. Many workplaces have an actual mentoring programme which staff can get involved in.

- Cultivate a positive attitude around your work. If you feel positive about your work then it will be more enjoyable. Thinking about gratitude and reflecting on the positives around your job can make life at work much better than being negative.

- Seek out fellow neurodivergent people at work. We really do form our own neurodivergent 'culture'. Being around neurodivergent 'family' at work can make your working life so much better.

- If you have mental health issues or stress, seek help for this, either from an existing clinician you are seeing (psychologist, etc.) or from a support service at your workplace if they have one. There is no shame in asking for help with mental health issues and not getting help can have serious consequences.

- If you have difficulty in prioritizing tasks and identifying which task is most important, you will need to ask for support, especially when you start a new job. If your job entails multiple tasks or components, ask your boss or work colleague to explain what tasks are a priority and what order they need to be done in.

- Ask for assistance at work from your manager or colleagues. This will help reduce anxiety and negative internal self-talk due to understanding and knowing what is expected of you.

- A good employer will welcome open and honest communication. And the same goes with anyone that you are asking assistance from. If you need to, ask your manager for clarification. When you are asking for clarification, this should not be viewed as a negative, but as a positive skill as you are taking the initiative to help yourself understand the expectations.

- Suffering in silence is detrimental to our wellbeing and by asking for help from a manager or colleague, we are inadvertently implementing self-care through reducing the unknown, reducing our anxieties and improving our self-esteem and self-confidence through doing our job well and meeting expectations. With open communication, it can positively identify prioritization of tasks and encourages us to schedule and plan for the day, week or month ahead.

- Many autistic people thrive on clear instruction, planning and having schedules. You can create your own task list to enable you to get all your work done and know what is coming up.

- If you have a task you are struggling with, you may know another person that is good in that area that you could ask to support you with completing the task. By suggesting this person to take on the job you are being offered, or finding potential solutions to the situation, you encourage good communication. Thinking of ways to resolve the situation by finding a suitable outcome will help get the job done.

Passions changing

Some autistic people have one passion which sustains them for their entire life. Many autistic people have a range of passions over time. In the context of using your passion to drive a career, the latter of these options can be a challenge. I (Yenn) have met a number of autistic people who are between passions. Their intense interest has concluded and they are yet to find another thing that sparks their joy. If you have got a job based on a passion but the passion wanes this can be a challenge. If you are between passions and you are no longer interested in the area you are working in there are a few options you might pursue:

- If the workplace is an inclusive one where you are liked and valued, we would consider staying there regardless of the topic of the work. A good workplace is an asset.

- If you are not respected and included at work, it is a much easier decision to make. In that situation it would probably be preferable to leave and find another job.

- Reflect on whether you like the elements of your job which aren't the topic of your previous interest. If you enjoy the work anyway then probably staying there is a good idea. If not, maybe consider changing your career.

- Changing jobs is a stressful process. Give your decision around what direction to take following your loss of interest a lot of care and do not rush your decision.

Leadership and mentorship to others

After a while in your job, you are likely to be highly proficient and have knowledge and wisdom to share with others, autistic people and neurotypical colleagues alike. Some workplaces offer formal mentoring programmes to staff. If your workplace does this, it might be something to consider. As you progress in a job you will gain skills and probably the respect of your colleagues and managers and any staff you might be supervising as well. There is no reason that autistic people shouldn't be mentors or leaders. In fact, some autistic people are great at leadership.

Author Yenn supervises a staff member in their job and Yenn's own manager has commented that Yenn is an excellent manager.

Career advancement

There is a stereotype around people with disability – including autistic people – in the workplace which states that giving a staff member with disability a job is somehow doing them a big favour. This view states that people with disability should not seek promotion or advancement because they should be grateful to get a job in the first place. This of course is complete nonsense, and ableist nonsense at that. There is also the view that autistic employees specifically can't be managers.

Author Yenn has been promoted twice in their career and is now a middle manager. Yenn is highly sought after at work for their understanding of the subject matter and their diligence and work ethic. Most of Yenn's managers in the past 15 years they have been in the job have appreciated Yenn's work. Autistic people have as much right to career advancement as anyone else does. An employer hires staff to do the job, not to provide some kind of charity for disabled staff! If you are in a job, you have the right to seek career advancement regardless of disability, gender, sexuality, race or anything else. There is no reason at all that you cannot advance your career.

Looking to the future – what does your career hold in store?

A career is an amazing journey. From our first foray into employment to retirement, there are many opportunities and experiences. We learn from our jobs or business and if your job or business relates to your passion, then the chance is that you will be a significant expert in the field by the time you get to retirement. In fact, if you are working on your passion you may not want to retire at all! You can't tell where your career will take you. One way to approach your career is to view it as an adventure. There will be twists and turns (metaphorically) and you might find yourself going places you didn't expect. Having a career that you enjoy and that relates to your passion rather than doing a job you don't have a lot of investment in has a range of positives – for your mental health and your sense of agreement and motivation. You probably won't spend every day of your career filled with delight and engagement – in fact, it is pretty likely that won't be the case. Even 'dream jobs' have elements that aren't very dreamy! But if you keep your career focused on your passions then it is highly likely you will remain engaged and committed to your work throughout your career. You never know where you will end up, career-wise. It really is an adventure.

Conclusion

We hope you have found this book helpful. We wish you all the best in your career journey and hope you find a role that aligns with your interests and a place to work where you are included, respected and accepted and where your passions are an asset. Autistic people really do work in every industry and every job. Autistic people use their passions to drive their careers and that is a good thing. There is a stereotype of an autistic university professor who is the world's foremost – and possibly only – expert on a very specific topic. That stereotypical professor is following their passion and has turned it into a career. And it definitely isn't just in the realm of stereotypes for autistic people to follow their passion and turn it into a meaningful career. Go forth and be amazing and change the world with your intense interest!

You are the CEO of your life (metaphorically). The CEO does not control the economy in which their company operates, but they do control what decisions they take in response to the economy. In other words, you probably can't change the world you live in, but you can decide what to do in response to what is happening in your life. This is definitely a good way to approach employment. You have some amazing skills and your interests may well make you a sought-after employee or successful business owner. The deficits view of autism is all about saying what autistic people can't do and shielding them from anything even slightly challenging. However autistic people can do amazing things and that includes at work. The barriers autistic people face in employment reflect the world we live in, the assumptions, misconceptions and stereotypes which drive people's views. As autistic people we – you – can smash those stereotypes and biases. By following your passion and using it to drive your career you are challenging and disproving those unhelpful biases and stereotypes. Your career isn't just a positive for you but for all the other autistic people out there too.

With much strength and respect, two passionate autistics, Barb and Yenn.

Glossary/Language

Ableism
Ableism refers to discrimination against people because they have a disability or health condition. It can be described as being like racism but against people with disabilities.

Autistic/person with autism
Some people say 'I have autism' and some say 'I am autistic'. These are called 'person-first language' and 'identity-first language'. Neither one is 'wrong'; they are both ways in which autistic people refer to themselves which reflect their identity as an autistic person. The authors of this book use identity-first language ('I am autistic'), but it is up to each individual how they choose to be described.

Disability and autism
Some people see autism as a disability. In terms of accessing support this can be a very useful way to view it. Autism is 'officially' a diagnosis in the diagnostic literature, but many autistic people do not see it as a disability, more a difference.

Disclosure
In the context of work, disclosure relates to your decision to tell your manager and/or colleagues that you have a disability or

health condition. There are pros and cons around disclosure and it is something which requires consideration and reflection.

Resume

Your resume is something to be provided to a potential employer as part of a job application process. Your resume lists your skills, previous work (if you have some), your educational qualifications and your attributes. This helps an employer decide whether you might be suitable for the job you applied for.

Skills

Skills covers a wide range of attributes which enable people to not only perform their work but also to manage life outside of work. There are literally thousands of skills that people can have. Some skills you can acquire, while others you are born with.

Work ethic

Work ethic describes a person's attitudes to their work. A person with a good work ethic is someone that cares about their work, wants to do things correctly and takes responsibility for what they do in their job. Managers are very keen on their staff having a good work ethic.

Workplace modification/accommodation

These are things which your manager/employer can put in place to make life easier for employees who are autistic or have disabilities or health conditions. Examples of workplace modifications for an autistic staff member would include things like removing bright lighting at their workstation, allowing them to work from home or making the workforce fragrance free. In many countries employees have the legal right to access workplace modifications if they need them.